TRUTH AND EXISTENCE

Original Text established and annotated by **Arlette Elkaïm-Sartre**

Translated by **Adrian van den Hoven**

Edited and with an Introduction by **Ronald Aronson**

JEAN-PAUL SARTRE

TRUTH AND EXISTENCE

The University of Chicago Press / Chicago and London

Originally published as *Vérité et existence*. © Éditions Gallimard, 1989

The University of Chicago Press, Chicago 60637
The University of Chicago Press, Ltd., London
© 1992 by The University of Chicago
All rights reserved. Published 1992
Paperback edition 1995
Printed in the United States of America
09 08   6 7 8

ISBN: 0-226-73523-0 (paperback)

Library of Congress Cataloging-in-Publication Data

Sartre, Jean Paul, 1905–
    [Vérité et existence. English]
    Truth and existence. / Jean-Paul Sartre ; original text established
and annotated by Arlette Elkaïm-Sartre ; translated by Adrian van den
Hoven ; edited and with an introduction by Ronald Aronson.
        p. cm.
    Translation of: Vérité et existence.
    Includes bibliographical references and index.
        1. Knowledge, Theory of.   I. Elkaïm-Sartre, Arlette.
    II. Aronson, Ronald, 1938–   III. Title.
B2430.S33V4713   1992
121—dc20   92-5889

CONTENTS

INTRODUCTION
THE ETHICS OF TRUTH

Ronald Aronson

Opening *Truth and Existence*, written in 1948 and post-humously published in 1989 by Sartre's adoptive daughter, Arlette Elkaïm-Sartre, we find ourselves in the midst of a controversy before turning a page. Elkaïm-Sartre's preface begins and ends with a statement by Sartre, about his search for a contemporary morality, that does not appear in the text of the work itself but only in the notes that followed *Truth and Existence* (p. 81 below). The statement, and the notes, are from a "new outline"—clearly not for *Truth and Existence*, but for a work on morality and history related to the ethical project with which Sartre was wrestling, unsuccessfully, during these years. According to the "new outline" Sartre would "try to elucidate the choice that a man can make of himself and the world in 1948." Writing about *Truth and Existence* in *Les Temps Modernes* not long after the French edition was published, Juliette Simont criticizes Elkaïm-Sartre for falsely advertising a work which is really about Sartre's "ontological theory of truth," perhaps thus trying to make it appear as a more attractive and saleable book on morality. She worries about an eventual "moral" deviation of the book brought about by Elkaïm-Sartre's preface and ethical-political concerns, but she is relieved that Sartre has foreseen and pro-

The author wishes to thank Walter Skakoon, Adrian van den Hoven, Leo Fretz, and Hazel E. Barnes for their kind and insightful assistance. The first draft of this introduction was presented before the Groupe d'études sartriennes in Paris.

tected himself against such distortions by his note, below on page 8: "A long time ago we got rid of our grandfathers' ghosts. We should now get rid of our great-grandchildren's ghosts." Meaning, as the reader will see in the text's opening and closing pages, that we cannot control what those who follow us will make of our actions.

Indeed, as if to make matters worse (although Simont does not mention this), Elkaïm-Sartre widely separates the two sets of pages that deal with these issues—exploring the difference between "historialization" and "historization"—and gives the place of honor, the book's first pages by Sartre himself, to the set that falls outside the text proper, and that contain what seem to be notes about history and authenticity (pages 1–2 below). As discussed in the "Note to the Reader" these thoughts, which echo Sartre's speculations in the project for a *Morale* that produced the *Notebooks for an Ethics*,[1] have less to do with the first pages of *Truth and Existence* than they do with Sartre's remarks in the final pages of the text; they clarify these remarks and might have fit better immediately after them. As Elkaïm-Sartre has arranged it, however (and we have reproduced this order below), these become Sartre's opening reflections on history. As such they are well-positioned to affect our reading of the text, inasmuch as they frame the discussion of truth which is the heart of *Truth and Existence* and so help to accentuate the "'moralization' of a text that does not deal with morality."[2]

Indeed, once the reader enters the text proper, s/he will enter well-known ground, the Sartre of *Being and Nothingness* asking his next set of questions, in familiar language. What is truth, according to Sartre? Even without having turned a page of *Truth and Existence*, many students of Sartre would have been able to project the outlines of a viable existentialist epistemology. It would have meant filling in the blanks he left us, basing our projections on more than an inkling of what this theory should include: an ontology of truth in terms of the play of for-itself and in-itself; an insistence on the central role of human action; Sartre's own efforts to link his thinking of the prewar years and of *Being and Nothingness* with his politicization and his later radicalization, indeed, his growing practical and theoretical preoccupation with history; and perhaps some attention to the question of intersubjectivity posed, but not resolved, by *Being and Nothingness*, namely how one particular for-itself arrives at a truth agreed to by the other. In *Truth and Existence* Sartre doesn't disappoint us: each of these themes receives elaboration.

But, as we look closely at the text itself, it becomes clear that it contains much more than an ontology of truth. If the word appears on every page, Sartre winds up saying relatively little directly about truth in this work, and in fact much of the text focuses on *ignorance*. Sartre introduces ignorance as a major theme on page 18, and then, after laying the foundation over the next several pages, begins a close discussion of it on page 28 that continues until virtually the end of the text. The sole characteristically Sartrean phenomenological description is devoted to a woman, T., who avoids becoming conscious of having tuberculosis and thus plunges into bad faith. But Sartre does not attempt a systematic description of truth, and we would search in vain for a detailed discussion of the processes of intuition or verification, or an exploration of any other traditional epistemological concern. Rather, in the pages below we will find not only an ontology of truth but also, and perhaps more important, a line of discussion that again and again opens onto the kinds of questions about freedom, action, and bad faith for which Sartre became celebrated—that is, *moral* questions. So much so that, without endorsing Elkaïm-Sartre's way of combining or arranging materials, I cannot agree with Simont's effort to separate truth from ethics. Rather, I invite the reader to explore a text that makes a major contribution to the *ethics of truth*.

Is this surprising? After all, the author is Jean-Paul Sartre. Characteristically, much of the text deals with human structures and behavior which are in fact *negative* towards the truth; indeed, much of *Truth and Existence* explores the argument that ignoring, although based on the primary ontological condition of ignorance (as is all knowledge), is an intentional act. In making this argument, it is worth noting, Sartre goes beyond the first meaning of the French *ignorer*, *not knowing*, in order to stress the meaning of *avoiding knowledge* through indifference or intention. Thus in stressing *ignoring* in the current English sense, as an act of will, Sartre has in mind an action aimed at *avoiding* or *hiding* an aspect of the truth. In other words, ignoring suggests a form of bad faith. And so, at the heart of *Truth and Existence* we find an explanation of ignorance as choice, analyses and phenomenological descriptions of behavior seeking to avoid the truth, and explorations of their *why*. It is Sartre at his most provocative: his study of epistemology, based on ontology, becomes a work on morality.

Sartre in 1948

A nonepistemological epistemology that turns more on discussions of ignorance as bad faith than of knowing: such paradoxes situate this posthumous manuscript in 1948. At this time Sartre was creating and riding the high tide of existentialism with incredible energy, as we can see by a glance at his bibliography, which shows more entries for this year than any other of his career.[3] In Annie Cohen-Solal's breathless description, this was the time when the "engine room" was in full production, making Sartre "a very rich man" by publishing nonstop from 1946 to 1949:

> more than forty works in less than four years. The
> genres included lectures, essays, plays, articles, intro-
> ductions, radio broadcasts, biographies, philosophical
> speculations, screenplays, songs, novels, reports. The
> themes ranged from aesthetics, literature, ethics, poli-
> tics and philosophy to travel, art and music.[4]

If, in these years Sartre attained his full stature as playwright, political essayist and activist, and editor, and explored new areas as novelist and philosopher, it must be stressed that his outpouring had several thematically connected goals.[5] He sought to intervene politically on behalf of a radical conception of freedom; to work out the consequences for a number of areas of life and thought of this conception and the ontology on which it was based; to connect his idea of free-dom, and himself as its author, with history and society both as conceptions and as realities; to demand other intellectuals' political commitment; to explore the theme itself of commit-ment (and its evasion). It was a coherent, if complex, project, unfolding on numerous fronts, characterized by its intellec-tual and political bite, its energy and ambition, its synthesiz-ing power, and its extraordinary self-confidence.

And in the midst of this activity, Sartre writes *Truth and Existence*, exploring the consequences of his ontology for how and what we can know. It is well known that *Being and Nothingness*, published in 1943 during the German occupa-tion, ends with a series of questions for "a future work" which can be answered only "on the ethical plane."[6] Not a single problem about truth or knowing appears among the dozen questions with which the work closes, even though Sartre's ontology would lead naturally to asking about how *my* knowl-edge corresponds to the other's knowledge. In fact, *Being and Nothingness* is so little interested in such questions that the reader might wonder how the worlds inhabited by a plurality of separate and conflicting for-itselves could become *a* co-herent world.

This is one of the central questions often posed about Sartre's famous subjectivism, and in approaching it *Truth and Existence* tackles an important gap in Sartre's work. At the same time, the manuscript proper poses questions about intersubjectivity near the beginning (5–12) and ends with questions about history (75–80) that appeared with Sartre's politicization and radicalization and came more and more to preoccupy him in the late 1940s, leading eventually to *Cri-tique of Dialectical Reason* (1960), *The Condemned of Al-tona* (1958), and *The Family Idiot* (1972, 1973)—along with *The Words* (1963) the great works of the second half of his ca-reer. Still, his thoughts on these topics do not give the text its dominant tone. Interesting as they are, they remain largely abstract and tentative, and appear before and after surer and more detailed analyses more directly inspired by *Being and Nothingness*.

At first it might seem that the core of *Truth and Existence* hearkens back to Sartre's 1930s psychological writings—*The Emotions* (1939),[7] *Imagination* (1936), *Psychology of Imagination* (1940)—inasmuch as it explores yet another process of evading reality, sometimes in strikingly similar language.[8] After all, isn't he describing a specific act, similar to imagining or strong emotion, the choice of unveiling or not unveiling the truth, in order to show its possible motivation and, above all, its connection with what we know or do not know, or perhaps even ignore, about the world? But *Truth and Existence*, unlike these psychological writings ten years earlier, is not preparatory for, but draws its force from, the ontology and the theme of bad faith so painstakingly developed in *Being and Nothingness*. In fact, it often seems that in the pages below a supremely self-confident Sartre is *applying* his ontology, using it as a guide to illuminate yet another major question. Moreover, the stress of *Truth and Existence*, like all of his postwar works, is on involvement *in* the world. It has shed the ambivalence of his early psychological writings and speaks fully and positively on behalf of engagement with being.[9]

If its inextricably intertwined moral, ontological, and engaged character places *Truth and Existence* firmly as a post–*Being and Nothingness* philosophical work, its concern with the choice to evade responsibility recalls Sartre's plays of the same postwar years, especially *The Respectful Prostitute* (1946) and *Dirty Hands* (1948). Having securely laid the ontological (and psychological) foundations of bad faith, Sartre uses his dramatic skills to show such behaviors in action in his plays. He contrasts it with the wholehearted embracing of freedom, reality, and responsibility represented by a character like Hoederer.[10] At the same time, parts of *Truth and Existence* are closely related to key aspects of Sartre's controversial demand for politically committed writing (*la littérature engagée*) in *What Is Literature?* (1946–47). As we shall see, both works go beyond *Being and Nothingness* in giving a positive cast to, and suggesting a positive outcome of, our fundamental ontological project.[11] And both place a premium on the notion of *revealing* reality; in the one case this is the writer's essential task, in the other the nature of the experience that we call intuition.

These postwar works, different as they may be in purpose and occasion, turn fundamentally on the belief that consciousness is free to choose between evading its responsibilities and actively accepting them. Sartre's notion of choice, which exploded onto the French, and then the world, intellectual scene between 1946 and 1949, is the core concern of his most prolific period. It is the essential existential problem of virtually all his dramatic work. Indeed, it is his key political concern, just as it is the very heart of Sartrean moralizing. In other words, for Sartre, especially in these years, questions of politics, ontology, and psychology all turn on the central tension between our responsibilities and our temptation to evade them, between facing and hiding from reality. This project found its stride as Sartre was embarking on a political direction after the war. Thus even as Sartre was opening more and more towards a different set of questions about history and collective action, his characteristic moral passion reaches flowering in these years. This is refracted through, and reaches full force in, such terms as freedom, responsibility, revealing reality, and bad faith.

Sartre has no doubt that his unique combination of moral passion and these specific themes is both genuinely new and socially vital. Indeed, this powerful mixture makes existentialism such a sweeping cultural force and emboldens Sartre to try to reshape the cultural and political landscape. He creates a journal, *Les Temps Modernes*, which would be an intellectual pole for the various non-Communist new-Left currents in France; thus, as the Cold War sets in, he struggles, unsuccessfully, to create a third way between the capitalist West and the communist East. Thus, in the name of his key themes, Sartre does battle against the French bourgeoisie, anti-Semitism, the Communist party, colonialism, American racism, and the "spirit of seriousness." In the midst of these battles, this flourishing of ideas and energy, he writes *Truth and Existence*.

Basic Themes

Sartre's starting point, not surprisingly, is ontological. *Being and Nothingness* had discussed knowing in the context of the basic ontological project, namely, as an effort to make being be mine, of seeking to become both its creator and possessor. By making my thought true, by therefore making it thought by everybody, I try to make it become both mine and independent of me. This is an effort at appropriation, akin both to digestion and sexual appropriation, and as such is intrinsically frustrating.[12] At the outset of *Truth and Existence* Sartre treats knowing for its own sake, and in so doing emphasizes at least two new dimensions. First, truth is seen as the progressive unveiling (*dévoilement*) of being-in-itself by being-for-itself. Second, one individual's vision is given to another, who makes it his own in transcending it towards his own ends. Thus we enter history, in two ways: "truth temporalizes itself more, that is to say that it appears according to the categories of before and after" (18). In other words, being is revealed "across *all* human history" (7). Second, Sartre tells us that "judgment is an interdividual phenomenon" (7). Although it is one thing to see and another to judge, seeing and judging are intertwined. Because of this, "often I see only by indicating. Thus man sees for the other, or sees the already seen" (7). Which, after all, amounts to saying that truth is an intersubjective matter.

These are all new and important themes for Sartre, and, as I have mentioned, they frame *Truth and Existence* in a physical sense: the first pages, accented sharply by the notes with which Arlette Elkaïm-Sartre begins the book, deal with questions of history and intersubjectivity. Sartre then goes on to demonstrate the internal links between ignorance and knowledge. After exploring willful ignorance throughout most of the text, Sartre focuses its last quarter on "necessary ignorance." He brings the work to a close by exploring a special form of necessary ignorance: that I can never live my action as it will be seen afterwards, by others. This structural question, ultimately rooted in the self-other dialectic of *Being and*

Nothingness, is also an important part of the project for a *Morale* that resulted in *The Ethical Notebooks.* Thus the core of *Truth and Existence* is placed within concerns suggesting the dimensions of history and society so central to Sartre's political involvement and so important in his later work.

Within this frame, which points eventually toward the *Critique of Dialectical Reason,* Sartre continues his project of illuminating every human realm *as action.* Thus there is an essential continuity between *Truth and Existence* and Sartre's prewar psychological writings, for example, *Imagination* and *Psychology of Imagination,* as well as *Being and Nothingness.* In every case, Sartre's goal is to transform apparent passivity into activity, states into acts: to reveal human choice, freedom, and spontaneity at the center of psychology and ontology.[13]

How does Sartre go from ignorance as the condition of all knowledge—which he will describe as *necessary* ignorance—to choosing a conduct that ignores reality? Knowledge is based on the fact that nothing is given to me by the world, and everything must be grasped by me. As *Being and Nothingness* already indicated, action aims at what is *not yet,* whether it is a future state of being or whether it is "what I would want it to be" (20). This is the origin of *anticipation* as a central theme of revealing action. Anticipation "precedes sight and constructs it. . . . [It] thus functions as a measure and guiding schema of *vision*" (21–22). In anticipating, I can organize the in-itself in relation to my view: "I create what is" (22). It is important to not take the "what is" in an idealist sense, because at stake is an independent in-itself that is always given as already-being, as merely being revealed by the upsurge of the for-itself.[14]

What then is error? It is a negative verification of our anticipation: the tree I expect is not really a tree, but something else. "Indeed, in error, Being *is not* what we say it is . . ." (25). Thus truth always contains a risk of error. Besides, it is always in the process of being verified by practice, which never stops using its objects and anticipating them—thus risking and projecting. After sketching "that complex game of Being and Not-being" (21), Sartre insists that "error is necessary to truth because it makes truth *possible*" (26).

We might say, with Heidegger, that without freedom there is no truth. Beyond its other consequences described in *Being and Nothingness*, the upsurge of the for-itself entails new, connected possibilities: ignorance and knowledge, error and truth. "Ignorance conditions knowledge and is defined by it," says Sartre, "that is, both as possibility of knowledge and as possibility of remaining in ignorance" (28). The different possibilities go together, as Heidegger indicates in "The Essence of Truth." But Sartre's emphasis differs drastically from Heidegger's by its stress on individual choice. Thus ignorance, which always surrounds knowledge, is also free behavior. As such, it depends on will. "I must decide the truth and want it; therefore I am able to *not* want it" (27). Sartre continues: "The condition of there being truth is the perpetual possibility of refusing it" (27). Although his words resemble Heidegger's here,[15] his major concern over the next third of the text will be neither the historical nor the ontological denial of primordial being, but the individual's denial of his/her responsibilities.

Avoiding Truth

This is the theoretical starting point from which Sartre will describe the choice of letting Being "remain veiled." Throughout the text's ontological analysis of truth, Sartre's inflection contrasts sharply with the conflictual and negative tone of relations between the for-itself and the in-itself in *Being and Nothingness*. He now describes relationships between the for-itself and in-itself that are mutually affirmative rather than antagonistic or steeped in bad faith or hopelessness. Indeed, verifying behavior "necessarily presupposes a *taste for being*" (my emphasis, 28), and this taste seeks to hide nothing, to avoid nothing. Of course this positive relation has a basis in Sartre's ontology: the for-itself begins by unveiling Being, and only exists to make it appear. But, although he reaffirms that "Being is terrifying" (44), Sartre now sounds positively optimistic about man's quest for Being when he describes this "irritating and voluptuous proximity without distance of the For-itself to what is not itself" as *enjoyment*. (29)

The sexual interpretation of *jouissance* was already central to Sartre's discussion of knowing as "carnal appropriation" in *Being and Nothingness*.[16] This particular remark elaborates on a passage of *What Is Literature?* written shortly before *Truth and Existence*, in which the creation of an aesthetic object gives joy and enjoyment. There Sartre speaks of the "sovereign calm of aesthetic emotions," and equally of a "rigorous harmony between subjectivity and objectivity."[17] The world—the in-itself being unveiled—no longer appears to me at this moment as an obstacle or as a menace, nor as tool nor as "the infinite distance that separates us from ourselves."[18] In reading, the famous tension between for-itself and in-itself is momentarily suspended and, even if only on the aesthetic plane, we reverse the famous conclusion of *Being and Nothingness* that "man is a useless passion." Indeed, the reader freely renders himself passive by becoming spellbound by the story. "It is a Passion, in the Christian sense of the word, that is, a freedom which resolutely puts itself into a state of passivity to obtain a certain transcendent effect by this sacrifice."[19] Reading is a *successful* passion: "The man who is reading has raised himself to the highest degree."[20] In other words, the in-itself appears to the for-itself as "a world that is both *his* world and the external world."[21] As a result, according to *Truth and Existence*, we are able to "*assume* the world *as if* we had created it, to take our place in it, to take the side of Being (to side with things), to make ourselves responsible for the world as if it were our creation" (30).

Sartre goes on to speak of *loving the true*, of facing up to facts, even those that trouble us, of preferring "Being to anything else, even in a catastrophic form, simply because it *is*" (30). He gives practical and ontological reasons for this. Practically, it is absurd to wish to ignore the truth: our projects, whatever they may be, organize themselves around a specific unveiling of being. Thus, for example, marriage is based on fidelity, whose verification is always in process as an essential dimension of the mutual project of being married. Indeed, it would be self-contradictory to choose to remain ignorant of my wife's behavior, as described in La Fontaine's "The Enchanted Cup." There, the wives' acts and gestures remain hidden to their husbands, by the husbands' own choice. Sooner or later, the reality will strike them, and they will be its victims: in choosing ignorance, they have preferred chance to the action of revealing.

This denial of the fundamental project of unveiling has ontological consequences. In choosing to ignore reality, I reject my task of unveiling being. Therefore I contradict my very upsurge into the world. In ignoring unrevealed being, I try to impute a lesser being to it. But this is impossible: in reality, I can only diminish my relationships with the world, as Sartre has described in his psychological works. Imagination and emotion were ways of fleeing from the world and my instrumental relationship to it, and in so doing I degraded myself. "Ignorance," he now says in *Truth and Existence*, "is the decision to let Being collapse" (33). I try to wash my hands of it.

A tubercular woman, T., chooses to not go to the doctor because she wants to ignore a danger of which she is conscious. If the existence of her illness were to be confirmed, it would give her new responsibilities; because verification involves revealing being, whoever verifies takes responsibility for an aspect of reality and becomes its accomplice. "T. refuses to take responsibility for allowing into the human world what has only the embryonic existence of a subterranean and nocturnal world. She refuses to choose herself as tubercular and to freely create tuberculosis" (34). Her denial changes nothing in the coughing, the spitting of blood, the fever, except that these are not lived for themselves. Each symptom is isolated from the other without being *seen* as such. But in letting tuberculosis kill her, T. will become passive, ignorant, without responsibility, victimized by chance. All the while she has fled her freedom, because "the fear of truth is fear of freedom" (34).

Of course some ignorance is necessary. We have to choose to ignore one part of reality in order to know another part of it, because all knowledge begins in ignorance and remains surrounded by ignorance. Nevertheless, it is still a matter of choice for T. to become absorbed in pursuing a particular activity, for example, in demonstrating her dramatic skills, and consequently to not have enough time to visit the doctor. This choice would amount to pursuing a hysterical distraction. In such an evasion, consciousness, trying to forget what it fears, plays at suppressing awareness of the disease, to the point of death. In reality, in suppressing our consciousness of the disease, we deaden ourselves and flirt with the state we fear most: the ignorant person "takes the point of view of death out of fear of death" (38).

All this returns us to bad faith: T. pretends to be controlled by destiny and fatality as she tries to evade her responsibilities before the fact of having tuberculosis. At the same time, the ignorant person becomes totally preoccupied by the suppressed truth. Tuberculosis is "the organizing theme of her innermost events." "But at the same time this theme constantly has a lesser being than Being. It is my anxiety's noema, a sign's signification, the correlative of an imagining act" (40–41). In this increasingly complex game, I deny my transcendence, I lie to myself, I render myself impotent: "in order to confer a lesser being on what threatens me, I confer a lesser freedom on myself" (41).

To explain why we are terrified by Being, Sartre returns to the relationships of the for-itself and the in-itself sketched in *Being and Nothingness*, and stresses the fact that Being *is terrifying*. By its very nature it is, after all, a rejection of my existence. It is *de trop*—superfluous—and it makes me, too, feel myself to be *de trop*.[22] Being is characterized by its absolute impenetrability, mystery, and "icy coldness," by being irreparable, unable to be recovered. It confronts me as an enemy, as a demanding thing, as an unchangeable condition, as pitiless. All this is entailed by its character of *being-there*. I can never change what it already is; my freedom is limited to the perpetual ambiguity of assuming responsibility for what I have neither created nor wanted. But in order to exist, consciousness must reveal this particular being and no other—this is its very condition of existence in a world of given and objective demands. That is, it is a choice without choice. In therefore affirming the original ontological tension and demands, Sartre suggests in fact the reasons why consciousness seeks to rebel against the necessity of its very upsurge—that it be conscious of, and responsible for, a reality it did not create.

The upsurge always happens as a particular project. I lose myself in the world of *means-imperatives*, crushed by the necessity of accumulating means to realize my ends, and by the weight of the means. Ignorance is a rebellion that aims at rejecting this perpetual labor of the world of means; but since freedom is labor, ignorance is therefore the rejection of freedom itself. In choosing ignorance, I want to create without working, that is, to make my desire "the universal motor of creation." I try to suppress the independence of being and reconstruct it as an extension of my mind, indeed, to have no further responsibilities except towards myself. Therefore ignorance tries to reinstall the Hegelian absolute subject as pure consciousness producing its own world.

In a series of brief and provocative reflections, Sartre goes further in his analysis of fleeing the act of verifying and describes three final modes of behavior towards truth, namely, innocence, contemplation, and abstract knowledge. Like ignorance, innocence chooses to not be responsible for the world. But the innocent one, protected from the world's ugliness (perhaps as a symbol of a lost childhood for which we are nostalgic), becomes a wise person in our eyes whose ignorance is preferable to a scientific and technological society's knowledge.

The story of Adam and Eve gives us another aspect of ignorance: the passive contemplation of a truth "already fully constituted *before us*" (56). It breaks the relationship existing between truth, our freedom, and our unveiling action. We have nothing to do with verification: truth is given to us by "the existent qualified to make the True exist" (56), that is, God, or perhaps even Hitler or Stalin; or indeed by those scientific authorities who "give" us such menacing truths as atomic energy. In making them into absolute and "unveiling" subjects, in criticizing them for the truths that they force us to accept, in forgetting that all verification is always in progress, we hide from ourselves *our own responsibility* to make the truth exist.

These forms of bad faith can lead us to the act of knowing without verifying, without seeing, without unveiling Being through intuition. We become absorbed in activities like reasoning—abstracted from experience—and in discourse that denies to intuition its "fundamental revealing value" (58). The person pursuing abstract knowledge *"reasons* not because he does not see but *in order not to see"* (58). This is the final component of Sartre's description of ignorance: in choosing abstract knowledge we are *absent* "out of fear of Being-in-itself."

What Is Truth?

So far I have sketched some of the main themes the reader will find in *Truth and Existence*. In the final pages Sartre details "necessary ignorance"—the fact that much of being necessarily remains in the dark, the other side of the coin. Therefore each verification is a choice to limit oneself, each piece of knowledge contains its finitude, and no historical act is able to see itself in the objectivity it aims at. Like all the analyses of *Truth and Existence*, these are simultaneously brief, clear, and insightful. And they lead us back to the heart of the entire Sartrean epistemological undertaking. I have suggested that Sartre gives us neither a detailed description of truth nor a sketch of verification. In fact, Sartre gives us these only by contrast, when speaking of ignorance. The explicitly epistemological themes of *Truth and Existence* are the other side of the coin, usually appearing between the lines of what Sartre actually says. The moralism that animates the whole text is based on a theory of truth that remains implicit most of the time, and which only furtively lets itself be seen. This vision draws us into some of the unresolved problems of Sartrean epistemology.

"What is the criterion of truth?" Sartre asks. "There is no

doubt on this point: it is *Being* as presence" (61). But what does he mean by *presence?* "Everything starts with sight and ends with sight (intuition)" [*Tout part de la vue et aboutit à la vue (intuition)*] (13). But does "sight (intuition)" mean sense-perception, or is it the more complex and sophisticated processes of either sense-perception (guided by a theoretical construct that renders being "as it is") or of creating and "seeing" (that is, grasping intellectually) the theoretical construct itself? Since he has already referred to "Galileo's *insight*" ["*la* vue *de Galilée*"] (p. 6), it would seem that Sartre has in mind not bare sense-perception but the more complex and sophisticated process of perception aided by instruments and guided by a theory. Indeed, Galileo's insight went contrary to the evidence of unaided perception. To see, then, may be to see an aspect of material reality, but it is to be guided by the vision of an individual who is able to *unveil* it for us using whatever perceptual and theoretical aids are available. No matter what the qualifications may be, Sartre has in mind a direct—therefore individual, therefore absolute, but nonetheless true—vision of the unveiled being. Based on Galileo's experience I can have my own personal experience, but this is not at all "a non-revelatory and purely subjective epiphenomenon" (67). Rather it is at one and the same time *my* truth, "truth become for the other," and universal truth. It always begins with an individual subject who has this direct experience of Being—even if the experience includes my history, environment, character, "a certain horizon of values, ends and significations" (65). Thus even if my truth springs from "the declining petty bourgeoisie and its projects, it is an absolute revelation and absolutely transmits Being" (67).

Thus truth is not found in statements; it has nothing to do with any intellectual or linguistic structure. To better understand this we must situate Sartre's individualization of truth in relation, for example, to epistemological approaches that would have us state truth, or find it in a mediated form, or construct it from intersubjective relationships. Truth is unveiled Being, characteristically accompanied by an "*il y a*"—"there is." Thus the Sartrean theory verges on a kind of absolute realism—the object is there, awaiting its unveiling, until we do so, and *see it*. At the same time Sartre's theory flirts with a kind of absolute intuitionism; at its heart are not statements about Being but rather seeing the object, directly and immediately. And yet at the same time Sartre's theory verges on a kind of absolute subjectivism; its pivot is *my* intuition and the intuition of each one of us, individual consciousnesses all.

But since truth is a direct and active vision of Being, how do we distinguish those aspects of my vision which are mine from those belonging to the specific being itself that is known; what we usually call the subjective components of the experience from the objective? For Sartre this traditional question does not seem to exist; he seems never to doubt that he can have it both ways, namely, that truth is given absolutely and directly in subjective intuitions, and that it is generally and objectively true and binding. Moreover, his theory of intuition never poses the question of how such a vision is prepared, which we find both in Descartes and in phenomenology. Sartre is concerned instead about another, related, question: if intuition includes a direct vision of being, how do I communicate this to others? Even if, as Marx says, this vision can be explained starting from a given social situation, it would be able to be "absolute revelation" that "absolutely transmits Being." But how to transmit it? Statements have a role in the process; with them I invite the other to see my personal vision, to make it into his/her equally personal vision. But in so doing s/he transcends my vision: "by transcending the *vision* and the *statement* towards my own ends, I make an object of them on my part and a *truth* precisely in the sense that truth is the objectivity of the subjective: Galileo's *insight* becomes law" (6). One person's vision becomes another's, and objectivity emerges in the very process that *steals* my vision from me. "I point out the object to him and he looks at it. He looks at it on the tip of my finger. But from then on, the object develops a dimension of being which escapes me a priori" (65). As for him, he sees this red flower from "another system of truth" (65). Thus in the very intersubjective process of its becoming objective, my truth receives an external limitation that makes it into something that is *no longer my truth*. Obviously, the presence of others adds nothing to my own vision and in fact they limit it. Indeed, as we have just seen, the *Mitsein*[23] may be an obstacle to direct vision, insofar as statements communicated from one person to another replace an individual's direct vision, and some people prefer to accept the dead and abstract truth of statements rather than experience it for themselves.

According to Sartre there is never any question that universal truth exists (and this commitment to an "absolute revelation" that "absolutely transmits Being" distinguishes him from the postmodernists), but as presented linguistically it is only a "pure abstract statement" (67). It is communicated in an invitation: "the pure index of a permanent possibility, valid for everyone, of freely realizing a certain unveiling" (67). In other words, I invite you to see what I have seen. Does this entail the same unveiling for everyone? Not at all, because each of us has a different character, personal history, bias, etc. Still, the fact remains that even if our perspectives differ, we all reveal the same being. Thus, as Sartre argues in *What Is Literature?*, a work that might be taken as a companion text to *Truth and Existence*, the writer can reveal a social world that the reader refuses to see. I as writer can avoid my responsibility to reveal our common world; you as writer can invite me to participate in an unveiling that shows me the world as it is and demands that I take responsibility for it. In both works Sartre seems to be saying that, epistemologically speaking, our individual visions, our unveilings, are true in an absolute sense: that is, they both reveal being as it is (or social reality in the case of *What Is Literature?*), and in so doing every one of us experiences it in a direct and immediate way that demands that we personally take responsibility for it. How can I know that what I see in this way is so? Only by intuition, that is, in the direct and personal experience of the subjectivity that wills to see reality. How can I verify that this is so? Only by offering it to others, as a gift. And as soon as they experience it themselves, they go beyond my truth.

Proof, if we may use that word, is based on good faith towards Being, the choice to see it; therefore it turns on the will to see Being, to refuse ignorance, and to take responsibility for what we have seen. Beyond this, no proof is necessary, because truth depends on each individual's direct intuition: *il y a.*

As we already know, one of the central themes of Sartrean bad faith is wanting to hide from or avoid the truth, or refusing to take responsibility for it. What matters in the Sartrean ethics of truth is not really intelligence, or rigorous proof, or reasoning, because in fact it is really not difficult to see what is. Granted, truth is never merely given to us, it takes work. But Sartrean truth still demands no explanation; without blinding ourselves through ignorance—a deliberate choice expressing a specific denial of reality for specific reasons—we all would see reality.[24]

Sources

I have laid special stress on what I regard as the most interesting and striking theme of *Truth and Existence*, namely the act of avoiding truth, and on its epistemological underpinnings, especially Sartre's simultaneously individualist and intuitionist, yet absolutist and objectivist, theory of knowledge. What are the sources of Sartre's approach to knowledge? One source appears in Sartre's very first philosophical and psychological writings, his first published steps of self-clarification in the 1930s. Ten years later Sartre writes *Truth and Existence* with Heidegger's "The Essence of Truth" very much in mind. Both most deeply and most immediately, then, the work takes shape under the influence of phenomenology.

We can see Sartre's view of knowledge emerge in his initial encounter with Husserl and Heidegger, as he was finding his philosophical bearings. For the young Sartre, phenomenology offered a way into the world that the idealism of his teachers, such as Léon Brunschvicg, had rendered inaccessible. As recounted delightfully by Simone de Beauvoir, his discovery of phenomenology came in the spring of 1933:

Raymond Aron was spending a year at the French Institute in Berlin and studying Husserl simultaneously with preparing an historical thesis. When he came to Paris he spoke of Husserl to Sartre. We spent an evening together at the Bec de Gaz in the Rue Montparnasse. We ordered the specialty of the house, apricot cocktails; Aron said, pointing to his glass: "You see, my dear fellow, if you are a phenomenologist, you can talk about this cocktail and make philosophy out of it!" Sartre turned pale with emotion at this. Here was just the thing he had been longing to achieve for years—to describe objects just as he saw and touched them, and extract philosophy from the process. Aron convinced him that phenomenology exactly fitted in with his special preoccupations: bypassing the antithesis of idealism and realism, affirming simultaneously both the supremacy of reason and the reality of the visible world as it appears to our senses. On the Boulevard Saint-Michel Sartre purchased Lévinas's book on Husserl, and was so eager to inform himself on the subject that he leafed through the volume as he walked along, without even having cut the pages.[25]

The key to phenomenology, as Sartre would construe it, is the idea of intentionality. The intentionality of consciousness offers a way out of the "digestive" philosophies of both realism and idealism. Brunschvicg, Lalande, and Meyerson, according to Sartre, sought to make all objects into "contents of consciousness," whereas phenomenology postulates a radical difference between consciousness and the things *of which* it is consciousness. Consciousness *aims* at or *intends* [viser] objects *outside it*. Thus consciousness is guaranteed its absolute spontaneity—by removing from it structures and preconscious constitutive processes—and the world's independent, external reality is preserved as well.[26] Consciousness is "clear as a great wind; there is no longer anything in it except for a movement to escape itself."[27] If it is *nothing*, consciousness exists only as it moves out of itself, towards objects. The consequence is striking:

> Thus, in a stroke, those famous "subjective" reactions, hatred, love, fear, sympathy, which floated in the foul-smelling brine of mind, tear themselves away: they are nothing but ways of discovering the world. It is things which are suddenly revealed to us as hateful, sympathetic, horrible, lovable. It is a *property* of this Japanese mask to be terrible, an inexhaustible, irreducible property which constitutes its very nature—and not the sum of our subjective reactions to a piece of carved wood.[28]

This means that I experience things *directly as they are*, not as mediated by subjective structures or constituted by subjective acts. And so Husserlian intentionality, as Sartre interprets it, frees us from a preoccupation with consciousness and "throws us onto the highway, in the midst of menaces, under a blinding light. To be, says Heidegger, is to be-in-the-world."[29]

Obviously Sartre is here embracing phenomenology's early call to look to "the things themselves" and rejecting Husserl's later interest in exploring preconscious constituting acts and processes as the source of those things. Sartre attacks the Husserlian notion of a transcendent ego, lying within or behind consciousness, and in so doing emphasizes the world's independence and objectivity. "Everything happens as if we lived in a world whose objects, in addition to their qualities of warmth, odor, shape, etc., had the qualities of repulsive, attractive, delightful, useful, etc., and as if these qualities were forces having a certain power over us."[30] The world's qualities belong *to the world*. "I pity Peter, and I go to his assistance. For my consciousness only one thing exists at that moment: Peter-having-to-be-helped. This quality of 'having to be helped' *lies in Peter. It acts on me like a force*" (my emphasis).[31] I am not driven to help Peter because of *my feeling:* "There is an objective world of things and of actions, done or to be done, and the actions come to adhere as qualities to the things which call for them."[32]

And so Sartre's ringing conclusion to his little essay on Husserl presents the basis for the theory of knowledge he will develop in *Truth and Existence:*

> Husserl has reinstalled horror and charm in things. He has returned us to the world of artists and prophets: frightening, hostile, dangerous, with havens of grace and love. He has cleared the ground for a new treatment of the passions which would be inspired by this truth which is so simple and so profoundly misunderstood by our people of taste: if we love a woman, it is because she is lovable. Thus we are delivered from Proust. Delivered at the same time from the "inner life": in vain would we seek, like Amiel, like a child who clings to the shoulders, the caresses, the coddling of our intimacy, since in the end everything is outside, everything, including ourselves: outside, in the world, among others. We will not discover ourselves in I know not what retreat, but rather on the road, in the city, in the midst of the crowd, thing among thing, man among men.[33]

As indicated above, in these 1930s writings Sartre sees himself as taking Husserl's insight in a Heideggerian direction: consciousness' intentionality is understood as being-in-the-world. But Sartre's being-in-the-world is not at all Heidegger's unitary, primordial phenomenon seen as underlying all other relations; although the for-itself and in-itself appear simultaneously in *Being and Nothingness,* Sartre stresses their difference, and describes the tension-filled relationship in which they bring about the world as we know it. Sartre's being-in-the-world, for all its Heideggerian overtones, means in the 1940s just what Sartre had described in the 1930s: that we are "rejected, abandoned by our very nature in an indifferent, hostile, and stubborn world. . . ."[34]

Having mentioned Heidegger in the 1930s as one of his two major philosophical inspirations, Sartre will later return to him, not only to study *Being and Time* as a prisoner of war in 1940–41 while working out the ideas for *Being and Nothingness,* but also to read "The Essence of Truth," published in French in 1948, as he was writing *Truth and Existence.* The reader will notice clear references to "The Essence of Truth" in the text, parallels to it in language and ideas, an apparent wholesale adoption of Heidegger's notion of truth as unveiling and of the bond between truth and freedom—and only a single explicit point of disagreement (concerning Heidegger's theme of *mystery,* p. 2). How far can we then say that Sartre writes *Truth and Existence* under the influence of "The Essence of Truth"?

We have already seen that from the beginning Sartre appropriates Husserl and Heidegger for his own purposes. He may borrow their terms, ideas, and whole lines of reasoning, but the outcome is a unique philosophy.[35] Sartre's stress on consciousness and subjectivity, the polar tension between the for-itself and the in-itself, make his being-in-the-world a much less stable and primordial entity than Heidegger's *Dasein* and its prior unity. Sartre's notion of bad faith may resemble Heidegger's inauthenticity, but ethics is clearly a more central and urgent matter for Sartre, and central to his ontology. After all, a radical notion of freedom and responsibility is Sartre's major philosophical contribution.[36]

And so with "The Essence of Truth."[37] If the publication of the French edition of "The Essence of Truth" provoked Sartre to write his own theory of truth, such a project, as I have suggested above, emerges naturally from within Sartre's philosophy, for Sartre's own reasons, and, in spite of similar terminology, leads in a radically different direction. When, for example, Heidegger speaks of *letting Being be* rather than hiding it, Sartre stresses the difference between actively *disclosing* Being and refusing to do so. For Sartre, to reveal Being makes us personally responsible for it—Sartre always speaks personally. Heidegger, on the other hand, is not interested either in the individual choice to reveal Being, or in the individual's ontological, psychological, or existential reasons for avoiding this. Rather, it is history that hides our being-in-the-world from ourselves: a massive philosophical reorientation is needed throughout Western society, rather than a comprehension of or confrontation with a given individual's bad faith. Sartre's equally ontological analysis points away from general philosophical problems and towards specific acts of evading responsibility by specific individuals, such as T.'s avoiding learning about her tuberculosis. Thus Sartre presents a sharp individual and ethical urgency, while Heidegger's critical focus is directed at the Western philosophical tradition, and his project is to reverse it. In this sense, Sartre's conception of truth, like the rest of his philosophy, is far more directly existential than Heidegger's.

Why Unpublished?

Truth and Existence is, the reader will find, a text that Sartre might well have published during his lifetime. It is clear, well-constructed, and often extremely well-written. Its arguments are sufficiently alive today to contribute significantly to contemporary discussions of knowing. After nearly a half-century it stands up every bit as well as Heidegger's "The Essence of Truth." And it makes an ideal text for discussions of truth, whether in introductory philosophy courses or elsewhere. Certainly it needs polishing, but it becomes confused only at one or two places (see especially p. 39). For most of the time it follows a single, if complex, path. The argument is lucid, its points are telling, and by any objective standard *Truth and Existence* deserved to be among Sartre's much-discussed texts of the late 1940s, "Materialism and Revolution," for example, or *What Is Literature?* It is easy to imagine *it* being debated just as fiercely as his other postwar writings. Therefore, a question: a completed, exemplary existentialist text, treating a theme its author considered important, abandoned by Sartre. Why?

We know that Sartre's interests shifted during this period. "After the war came the true experience, that of *society*."[38] Having laid the foundations of his philosophy during the 1930s and 1940s, he was now applying it to the world around him; having held himself aloof from politics during most of these years, he was now intervening in the issues of the day. Having explored questions of individual psychology and of ontology, Sartre was now creating political organizations, editing a journal, and thinking generally and specifically about morality and history. His project of writing an ethics, embodied in the *Notebooks for an Ethics*, reflects, and was a casualty of, this period. In it Sartre sought to answer some of the decisive—and philosophically most vexing—questions left by *Being and Nothingness*, at the same time as he was beginning to explore the new dimensions of society and history. Built upon, but veering away from *Being and Nothingness*, the *Notebooks for an Ethics* expressed, but eventually gave way before, Sartre's need to more fully and systematically situate himself in history. After the war, "I abandoned my prewar individualism and the ideal of the pure individual and adopted the social individual and socialism. That was the turning point of my life; before and after. Before, I was led to write works like *Nausea*, where the relation to society was metaphysical. After, I was gradually led to write the *Critique of Dialectical Reason*."[39]

What Is Literature?, the *Notebooks for an Ethics*, and *Truth and Existence* were all written during the immediate postwar period, between the before and the after. *What Is Literature?* succeeded where the *Notebooks for an Ethics* failed because it moved Sartre, and his audience, from the before to the after, from *Being and Nothingness* to the *Critique*. In it Sartre effects a transition from the individual to society, from aesthetics to politics, from withdrawal into the imaginary to political commitment.[40] *Truth and Existence*, however, does not attempt such a transition. It stays far more solidly within the problematic of *Being and Nothingness* than either work, thus qualifying it both as an ontological theory of truth and as an ethics of truth. In other words, while it perfectly reflects the classical existentialist Sartre at the height of his powers (and fills a major lacuna in his work), Sartre may well have shortly afterward seen *Truth and Existence* as reflecting a perspective he was leaving behind—that of the writer, the asocial individual, the isolated person standing outside of history. Indeed, Sartre claimed that he realized during the very same period that his *Morale*, which contained far more of society and history than *Truth and Existence*, was becoming an idealist ethics, and so abandoned the project he castigated as a "writer's ethics."[41] Perhaps then Sartre concluded that this theory of knowledge was a "writer's conception of truth"—and so likewise left it unpublished?

To be sure, it contained significant indications of the thinking that was to follow. For example, below on page 44, the reader will find a note that Elkaïm-Sartre calls Sartre's "first formulation of a theme that will play an important role in the *Critique of Dialectical Reason*." In this note Sartre describes the "very meaning of work" and the "first *theme* of life in society" as "being in the world within a world *that refuses my existence.*" And then he mentions, as one of the subsequent points: "Antagonism of men and scarcity of goods. Ambivalence of social life. The other is he who shares my food with me and who steals it." This note is on the reverse side of the notebook page where Sartre says that "Being is terrifying." Thus we can see Sartre's thought on the one hand pointing back to his first formulation of intentionality, as described above (with its echoes of *Nausea* and *The Emotions*) and on the other hand pointing forward to scarcity and *Critique of Dialectical Reason*. Or, to put it more sharply, we can see the roots of scarcity in Sartre's first understanding of the nature of Being, as consciousness encounters it.[42]

Other ways in which *Truth and Existence* anticipates the *Critique* have been suggested by Leo Fretz.[43] These are found in the text and not the notes, in statements near the end of the text that are part of Sartre's discussion of historialization and historization, the first being my action as done for its own sake and intrinsic reasons, the second being my action as viewed by others. "But what must be understood is that it is in historialization that the concrete absolute, and the unveiling of truth to the absolute-subject, reside. The mistake is in seeing an epiphenomenon of historicity there" (79–80). And secondly, "we must make ourselves historical against a mys-

tifying history, that is, historialize ourselves against historicity" (80). In other words, historical truth is first of all *lived
history*, from the perspective of those struggling within it, not
from that of those who consider it from the outside and afterwards. The historical dialectic is first of all a subjective and
not an objective one, and historical truth must be pursued
from the point of view of those passionately involved in, and
even blinded by, history's struggles, not by those who consider these struggles from the point of view, say, of military
schools analyzing battles after the fact in order to determine
the "correct" strategy and tactics.[44] More generally, the opposition between living the dialectic from within versus being
acted upon from without is a central tension of the *Critique*
and animates the process that moves from praxis to the prac-
tico-inert and back.

According to another provocative suggestion by Fretz, "the
thesis of the counterfinality of matter in the *Critique* is already prepared" earlier in *Truth and Existence*, namely, its
discussions of means and ends on pages 1–2 and 69–80. These
reflections stress our inability to anticipate all the consequences of our actions. It is as impossible to simply derive our
results from the means we use as it is for our ends to automat-
ically produce their appropriate means. Freedom in the world
(as opposed to determinism on the one hand and idealism or
wishful thinking on the other) thus demands accepting the
fact that risk is inherent in all our actions. The risk, that is,
that things will not turn out as we intend them. Thus, in a
deep sense, all of my actions begin and end in ignorance, and
an "ethics of risk" (Fretz) must begin with the Socratic understanding that "I know that I know nothing." From here it is
a small step to Sartre's discussions of practico-inertia in volume 1 of the *Critique* and deviation in volume 2.

To be sure, these discussions appear in *Truth and Existence* at a level of abstraction that makes them hard to penetrate, and are further developed in the text's closing pages
only as an example that "will plunge us into the very heart of
this necessary ignorance" (75). The notes that Elkaïm-Sartre
has placed before the text touch upon the relationship be-

tween historialization, historization, and authenticity. Sartre does not yet possess the tools, or the point of view, to handle issues relating to counterfinality and history with full clarity and confidence; he will have both in the *Critique*. But even if these thoughts tend towards obscurity compared with the rest of *Truth and Existence*, the undeniable fact is that the text begins and ends with discussions that lead away from epistemology in the spirit of *Being and Nothingness*, and towards the more direct and concrete encounter with history and society that Sartre was to pursue in the 1950s, 1960s, and 1970s. More specifically, it provides the first formulations of that encounter's major themes.

Implications

Still, its location within the unresolved tensions of a decisive period in Sartre's career takes nothing away from the force of the work itself. And his radical theory of truth can help us to explain Sartre's great postwar fame, some of the characteristics of his writing, the strength of his invective, as well as, paradoxically, the absence of epigones of Sartre today. In his various and voluminous works, Sartre acted in accord with his words: unveiling reality, attacking all those whom he believed guilty of bad faith. Penetrating both communist and bourgeois rhetoric and hypocrisy, Sartre succeeded in unveiling decisive aspects of our world and in presenting dazzling insights. No argumentation, no reasoning against contrary positions, but description heaped on description, sometimes overwhelmingly, in page after page, volume after volume: in work after work he tried to present reality itself, self-evident and direct. And judgments on those who refused to see this reality. What is the connection between his famous condemnations and the theory of truth presented in *Truth and Existence*? Listen to the ringing conclusion of his most famous description of freedom:

> Thus, in the name of that will to freedom which is implied in freedom itself, I can form judgments upon

those who seek to hide from themselves the wholly voluntary nature of their existence and its complete freedom. Those who hide from this total freedom, in a guise of solemnity or with deterministic excuses, I shall call cowards. Others, who try to show that their existence is necessary, when it is merely an accident of the appearance of the human race on earth—I shall call scum [salauds].[45]

Vicious insult is an integral part of the Sartrean armamentarium—directed at fascists, racists, anti-Semites, bourgeois, supporters of colonialism. They are not merely politically or intellectually wrong, but deeply flawed morally as people who have embraced bad faith. If the peremptory and moralizing tone of Sartre's moral and political practice is notorious, I would stress the links between it and his indifference to the give-and-take of argument, his conception of truth as direct intuition of what is already *there*, the centrality of his theme of bad faith, as well as his theory of engaged literature. If, according to Sartre, ignorance begins with an act of will, it makes no sense to be patient, to reason, to develop an argument, to convince. Moreover, according to Sartre, if ignorance is a choice, it is a behavior that one must change first before succeeding in seeing the truth.

This may help us explain a remarkable phenomenon that at first glance seems totally unrelated to these questions: the striking absence of Sartreans after Sartre. Of course, he has left major ideas and themes, brilliant and powerful descriptions, marvelous works. In fact, we might say that in a sense the whole world has wound up accepting Sartre today: the idea of freedom as responsibility, his idea, has become a central thread of contemporary consciousness. Even so, today there are few people who identify themselves sufficiently with Sartre to be able to be called Sartreans. I think that the stress Sartre placed on intuition and on knowledge as will provides two reasons for this.

Without sketching the bases of a communicable objectivity, without an explicit method for reaching it and validating it, Sartrean intuitionism remains anchored in specific intuitions, *his* intuitions. Thus, if certain ideas of Sartre have aged, if others have been absorbed into the general consciousness— which is only natural—others appear idiosyncratic. We must ask if Sartrean philosophy would have fared better if Sartre had developed a method, an approach to knowing, evidence, and verification. The best we have is *Truth and Existence.*[46] What remains is a task for those who follow Sartre: to make this provocative and brilliant discussion of ignorance into a theory that is more complex, less moralistic, more nuanced, less simple, more developed—but which still bears his hallmarks and continues to stress the central role of will and intention, choice and action.

Notes

1. See *Cahiers pour une morale* (Paris, 1983), especially pp. 26–124; trans. David Pellauer, *Notebooks for an Ethics* (Chicago, 1992), pp. 20–117.

2. Juliette Simont, "Les Fables du vrai (à propos de *Vérité et Existence*)," *Les Temps modernes* (October-December, 1990): 225.

3. See Michel Contat and Michel Rybalka, *Les Ecrits de Sartre* (Paris, 1970); trans. Richard McCleary, *The Writings of Jean-Paul Sartre* (Evanston, Ill., 1974). Contat and Rybalka record 135 pages of entries for the 1945 period, compared with 92 and 90 for his next two most productive half-decades.

4. Annie Cohen-Solal, *Sartre: A Life* (London, 1988), p. 281.

5. See my review of Cohen-Solal, "Sartre: A One-Man Empire?" *The Jewish Quarterly* (Autumn, 1990): 32–35.

6. *L'Etre et le Néant* (Paris, 1943); trans. Hazel Barnes, *Being and Nothingness* (New York, 1956), p. 638.

7. Esquisse d'une théorie des émotions (Paris, 1939); trans. Bernard Frechtman, *The Emotions: Outline of a Theory* (New York, 1948).

8. Compare the following two passages. The first is from *L'Imaginaire* (Paris, 1940); *Psychology of Imagination* (New York, 1948):

To prefer the imaginary is not only to prefer a richness, a beauty, an imaginary luxury to the existing mediocrity *in spite of* their unreal nature. It is also to adopt "imaginary" feelings and actions for the sake of their imaginary nature. It is not only this or that image that is chosen, but the imaginary state with everything it implies; it is not only an escape from the content of the real (poverty, frustrated love, failure of one's enterprise, etc.), but from the form of the real itself, its character of *presence,* the sort of response it demands of us, the adaptation of our actions to the object, the inexhaustibility of perception, their independence, the very way our feelings have of developing themselves. This unnatural, congealed, abated, formalized life, which is for most of us but a makeshift, is exactly what a schizophrenic desires. (pp. 210–11)

In *Truth and Existence* Sartre writes:

It is not true that the schizophrenic prefers the dream because he appears there as a millionaire, an emperor, etc. He prefers the world of dreams because Being *is* in it only to the exact extent that it is revealed: he prefers the *poverty* of Being because Being is a *lesser being*, which is immediately reabsorbed in subjectivity and because between the desired being and the desiring being there is no intermediary. There is no doubt that we deprive ourselves of the satisfaction (of the desire), but this is deliberate because satisfaction is suppression of the desire and mystification. The world of dreams is a world of desire that wants to remain desire and let itself be announced by a being which is the exact counterpart of desire (p. 53).

9. For a discussion of Sartre's early list towards the unreal, see my *Jean-Paul Sartre—Philosophy in the World* (London, 1980).

10. Or, later, and victoriously, by the 1953 play *Kean* (Paris, 1954); trans. Kitty Black, *Kean, The Devil and the Good Lord and Two Other Plays* (New York, 1960).

11. Simont notes this positive character of *Truth and Existence* but ignores the sharp difference of approach and tone that makes it such a departure from *Being and Nothingness*. See Simont, "Les Fables du vrai," pp. 193–209

12. *Being and Nothingness*, 577–80.

13. See, for example, *L'Imagination* (Paris, 1937); trans. Forrest Williams, *Imagination: A Psychological Critique* (Ann Arbor, 1962). Of course this determination remains the thrust of the *Critique* as well, but now in intimate connection with history and society. See my *Jean-Paul Sartre—Philosophy in the World* and my *Sartre's Second Critique* (Chicago, 1987).

14. It is worth noting that these passages effectively reverse the argument of *Imagination* and *Psychology of Imagination*, which speak of perception as passive and stress the imagination's spontaneity.

15. See Martin Heidegger, "The Essence of Truth," in *Basic Writings*, ed. David Farrell Krell (New York, 1976).

16. See "'Doing' and 'Having': Possession," *Being and Nothingness*, pp. 575–600.

17. "Qu'est-ce que la littérature?" *Situations*, II (Paris, 1948); trans. Bernard Frechtman, *What Is Literature?* (New York, 1949), p. 53.

18. Ibid.

19. Ibid., p. 44.

20. Ibid., p. 45.

21. Ibid., p. 54.

22. The term is used in *Nausea* to describe Antoine Roquentin's startling insight into the real nature of existence (*La Nausée* [Paris, 1938]; trans. Lloyd Alexander, *Nausea* [New York, 1949]). Sartre's psychological writings, as well as his little essay on Husserl's intentionality, also take up the same theme of Being as terrifying.

23. Literally, "being-with." As Sartre absorbs this term from Heidegger, he means being "not in conflict with the Other but in community with him" (*Being and Nothingness*, p. 413). His first extended analysis of the *Mitsein* concludes: "The essence of the relations between consciousness is not the *Mitsein;* it is conflict" (429). His postwar writings, such as *What Is Literature?* and *Truth and Existence* explore more harmonious relationships. See my *Jean-Paul Sartre—Philosophy in the World*, pp. 129–36.

24. Juliette Simont unaccountably ignores this major theme of the text, and of Sartre's thinking in general, and focuses instead on the notion of truth in Sartre as being scarcely differentiated from fiction. Having rejected the connection between ethics and truth in the text, having given short shrift to Sartre's concentration on the act of ignoring (see her fleeting discussion of it on pp. 210–11), she also pays no attention to the unique intuitionism/ subjectivism/realism I have just described. Instead, with only a single reference to the text itself of *Truth and Existence*, she introduces fable, fiction, and drama into Sartre's notion of truth, using a famous discussion that appears much later, in volume 1 of *The Family Idiot*, along with an idea of coherence that appears nowhere in Sartre's text. This postmodern reading of Sartre is so radically different from what I have just described that I will simply present it and allow the reader to decide.

[According to the methodological principle discussed on p. 139 of *The Family Idiot*] if no further true synthesis is promised, conversely, no falsehood is purely false, and there is no longer anything but the perpetual rearrangement of a "verification" within which, as Sartre already wrote in *Truth and Existence*, we decide to call an "error" what is only a negative verification according to convenience and in a hierarchy which is itself false.

To a certain extent, all truth is a fable. And this is already the case in *Truth and Existence*. Indeed, after temporality, *the intermingling of the true and the false*—the process of *disguising* or of *simulation* by which truth is realized—can be considered as the second modality of the operation of truth. Return to the example of the tree in the night. Everything begins, we have seen, from the end as false-being, as non-being that is disguised with a borrowed being, and it is on this simulated being that the organization of being is traced: to see is to simulate, the vision of the tree "signifies that I imitate the vision of the tree" (22). In this sense nothing is less true than the truth; in the end it can only be the placing in coherence of a quid pro quo—the moment when the true being is given in "person" might not differ from a perfectly successful simulation, when the false-beings which are secondary ends enter into an agreement without objection [*consonance non grinçante*], and therefore verified, with the false-being of the original end. (199–200)

. . . If ignorance and bad faith are on the same plane for Sartre, if they are characterized by a "realizing comedy," how then can we understand in what ways truth and ignorance differ, inasmuch as truth also appeared to us to intrinsically contain a part of fiction or comedy? According to what criteria can simulation or the imaginary sometimes give way to the truth, and sometimes to the mechanical subjection to a role? Where is the dividing line?

We have there two kinds of syntheses differently mobilizing the imagination that crosses them, two functional placings in relation which, because they are nothing other than a function, only respond to criteria they give themselves. There are therefore only retrospective characterizations, but not norms of production. What would be this characterization? In the two cases there is game, comedy. The comedy of truth *plays with being itself*, interiorizes each in the other, a being and negation game—therefore is "true" since nothing outside evaluates it, since the only account it has to give is its own coherence; the comedy of bad faith *plays at being a being exterior to the game*, the café waiter, the actress in the theater—and can only be in default in relation to this transcendent being which immediately becomes pure imaginary and ineffective perspective, while the synthesis effectively disaggregates itself into a game lost to its coherence, mad alternation of brutal reality and inaccessible ideal: from the formless cough to the noble urgencies of theatrical art, from the dead hand to disinterested considerations on the aporias of sentimentality. In a sense nothing separates truth from bad faith or ignorance; nothing but a difference of accentuation in the way of playing with this nothing: game of being with nothing gone in the first case, game for being against nothingness in the second. Different distributions of the intensity of freedom. . . . (214–15)

25. Simone de Beauvoir, *The Prime of Life* (Cleveland, 1962), p. 112.

26. In *Being and Nothingness* Sartre's "ontological proof" states the following: "To say that consciousness is consciousness of something is to say that it must produce itself as a revealed-revelation of a being which is not it and which gives itself as already existing when consciousness reveals it" (p. lxii).

27. "Une Idée fondamentale de la phénoménologie de Husserl: l'intentionnalité," *Situations*, I (Paris, 1948), p. 30.

28. Ibid., p. 32.

29. Ibid., p. 31.

30. *La Transcendance de l'égo* (Paris, 1965); trans. Forrest Williams and Robert Kirkpatrick, *The Transcendence of the Ego: An Existentialist Theory of Consciousness* (New York, 1957), p. 58.

31. Ibid., p. 56.

32. Ibid.

33. "Une Idée," p. 32.

34. Ibid.

35. See my chapter, "The Source of Sartre's Thought," in *Jean-Paul Sartre—Philosophy in the World.*

36. In Heidegger's view, Sartre fails to delve deeply enough into being, wandering instead in the subject-object dichotomy rather than exploring its source. See "Letter on Humanism," *Basic Writings.*

37. This 1930 lecture appears within a larger and more complex trajectory, only part of which Sartre was aware of. A close look at Heidegger's itinerary raises doubts about the secure, self-confident tone of "The Essence of Truth." For a discussion of the role of knowledge in Heidegger's career, see Charles B. Guignon, *Heidegger and the Problem of Knowledge* (Indianapolis, 1983).

38. "The Itinerary of a Thought," *Between Existentialism and Marxism*, trans. John Matthews (London, 1974), p. 34.

39. "Auto-portrait à soixante-dix ans," *Situations*, X (Paris, 1975); trans. Paul Auster and Lydia Davis, "Self-Portrait at Seventy," *Life/Situations: Essays Written and Spoken* (New York, 1977), p. 48.

40. This is why it remains a central text for understanding Sartre's development. See my *Jean-Paul Sartre—Philosophy in the World*, pp. 122–53.

41. See Contat and Rybalka, *The Writings of Sartre*, entry 49/187, pp. 228–29.

42. It is worth noting, however, that the other *shares with me* in this formulation. This theme is missing from the *Critique* in any more than a perfunctory way, and its absence is one of the sources of that work's problems. See my *Jean-Paul Sartre—Philosophy in the World*, pp. 265–70, and my *Sartre's Second Critique*, 234–41.

43. Fretz makes the following assertions, but unfortunately does not develop them, at the end of an unpublished paper, "La place de Vérité et Existence dans le développement philosophique de J.-P. Sartre" (Delft University of Technology: April, 1991).

44. Ibid., p. 26. The military-school analogy is Sartre's own. See *Critique of Dialectical Reason*, II: *L'Intelligibilité de l'Histoire* (Paris, 1985), pp. 15–19; and my *Sartre's Second Critique*, pp. 42–44.

45. *L'Existentialisme est un humanisme* (Paris, 1946); trans. Philip Maire, *Existentialism and Humanism* (London, 1948), p. 52.

46. The reader may be interested in "The Legend of Truth," a fragment of a larger manuscript of the same name written in 1929. This attempt at a literary and philosophical synthesis was published in *Bifur*, no. 8, June 1931, along with a section of Heidegger's *What Is Metaphysics?* It appears in Contat and Rybalka's *The Writings of Jean-Paul Sartre*, vol. 2 (Evanston, 1974), pp. 37–52. Contat and Rybalka discuss it in vol 1, pp. 42–43.

CONTEXTS

Arlette Elkaïm-Sartre

> And so I am searching for an ethics for the present. . . . I am
> trying to elucidate the choice that a man can make of himself
> and the world in 1948.

In the years that passed between the publication of *Being and
Nothingness* (1943), where Sartre announced the launching of
this project, and of the *Critique of Dialectical Reason* (1960),
Sartre reflected a great deal on this subject, reflections which
remained unpublished in his lifetime. What relationship was
there between his two major works? Should we consider the
second to imply an abandoning, whether temporary or not, of
the project announced at the conclusion of the first work, or
should we see the *Critique* as a necessary detour in order to
better achieve his initial goal of founding an ethics?

In 1983, three years after Jean-Paul Sartre's death, we published *Notebooks for an Ethics*, a collection of notes written
in 1947 and 1948. These notes make it possible to follow for a
period of time the course of his thought after *Being and Nothingness*. They deal specifically with the question of the *reign
of value* in ethics, as he posed this question to himself at the
end of this work while keeping in mind the concept of freedom that he formulated there: "is it possible for freedom to
take itself for a value as a source of all value, or must it necessarily be defined in relationship to a transcendent value which
haunts it?"[1]

1. *Being and Nothingness*, trans. Hazel Barnes (New York, 1956), p. 627.
(R. A.)

xliii

Written after the *Notebooks* in 1948, *Truth and Existence* allows the reader to continue following in Sartre's footsteps. As far as we know, it is the only one of his mature posthumous writings that is complete. It is a first draft, and on certain of the left-hand pages of the notebook in which he wrote (the side he used for making notes), he jotted down ideas to be developed later or to be integrated into a second draft. These notes, signaled by asterisks, here appear as footnotes to the text. (On the last page of his essay, after drawing a line, Sartre sets out a new outline for his ethics. We have included it as an appendix.)

In the process of constructing his ethics Sartre inevitably encountered the question of Truth from a particular point of view. He had already touched on the question in the *Notebooks*, where he examined specifically the Hegelian position on *truth as having become (la vérité devenue)*. A few months later he obtained *De l'Essence de la Vérité* ("The Essence of Truth"), a translation of a lecture by Martin Heidegger, which had just been published. It is possible that this essay, to which he makes numerous allusions, impelled him to write his own essay which he may have intended to publish one day. In fact, Sartre remains quite distant from Heidegger's thought because their objectives differ: the latter focuses on the truth of Being while the author of *Being and Nothingness* wants to evaluate the value of the concept of truth in the intersubjectivity of (human) existents, as his title indicates. He also criticizes the Heideggerian notion of *mystery* and the opposition it implies between two ethical realms.

It may be useful to acquaint readers first encountering Sartre through *Truth and Existence* with some salient elements of *Being and Nothingness;* the former is linked to it and can also be considered a *transitional work*. Sartre distinguishes between two regions of Being: being-in-itself, which is the being of any phenomenon, and the being of consciousness, which is for-itself. We can say nothing of being-in-itself except that it is; the being of consciousness, on the other hand, cannot be separated from what it is conscious of, and, thus, it is *nothing* in itself. Human-reality, insofar as it is characterized by consciousness, creates its essence through its acts; thus this essence is always to come. One of the characteristics of every human activity is to be unveiling and verifying. All thought, all practical action and behavior, imply a relationship with Truth. But where is the guarantee of Truth if, as is the case with Sartrean existentialism, we do not allow for the intervention of divine revelation, that divine gift of a notion of truth according to the needs and possibilities of human nature?

Moreover, man has a totalizing vocation vis-à-vis the Truth. But can he sustain this vocation, or does all truth remain fragmentary and relative? But relative to what? To an age? Besides, the meaning of these simple words "our age" is problematic and clouded in ignorance. And yet we must decide. If all relationships of man with a realm beyond him should be excluded, it would be pointless to conceive of an ethical human truth and, according to Sartre—because the problem is central to the writer—it might well be pointless to write. When I state publicly what I consider to be a truth, for whom is it a truth and for how long? My truth is simultaneously unveiling and gift to the other. It enlightens the person who receives it but according to his own subjectivity and historical circumstances, etc., and these are all matters which I do not control. Is the illumination of Being an absolute good or should I worry about its impact and the consequences of the evidence I provide, and hold myself responsible for what I do not know? To rediscover ourselves, we need a ground. Sartre returns here to the apparently irreducible oppositions of the relative and the absolute, the finite and the infinite, the one and the many, the particular and the universal. This text permits us to perceive why his project of wanting to found an ethics resulted in the *Critique of Dialectical Reason*, a radical questioning of the structures and meaning of History and the very tools used to reflect upon it.

Sartre wrote *Truth and Existence* in 1948, under the disturbing shadow of the Cold War. Nuclear war and the end of mankind through a third world war were current topics. The philosophical debate on the fate of the human adventure could be decided at any moment—whether it was seen as infinite progress, as having a necessarily catastrophic end, or as a definitive and absurd event (something which, by the way, he tried hard to stave off through his writings and acts).

"And so I am searching for an ethics for the present. . . ." This quest, traces of which persist into his last interviews, would have seemed quite out-of-date even a few years ago. Today, now that *the possibility that the world has become such that any kind of freedom is henceforth impossible in it*[2] again touches many a consciousness—but for other reasons; and now that ethics committees are springing up, Sartre's quest again makes him our contemporary.

2. It appears that this quote is an amalgamation of two phrases: the first appears below on pp. 71–72 (it is on p. 125 in the original French text); the second appears on p. 72 below (it is on p. 127 in the original). The first talks about "the possibility that the world renders freedom impossible"; the second argues "that the world can always render certain freedoms impossible (economic crises, slavery) and that it can become such (e.g., destruction of the world) that any freedom becomes henceforth impossible in it." (R. A.)

NOTE TO THE READER

This translation is based on the French edition as published by Gallimard in 1989. That edition follows Sartre's original manuscript in placing Sartre's notes on the left-hand pages facing the pages on which the notes are commenting. We have placed these notes at the bottom of the appropriate pages. Since he did not place note numbers in his text, but rather began each note directly across from the passage to which he was referring, we have used asterisks to mark the nearest sentence break to the original manuscript page being commented on. According to Arlette Elkaïm-Sartre, some of Sartre's notes appear to have been written later than the others, judging from the larger and more nervous handwriting; these were placed within brackets. The editor's and translator's notes will be found at the end of the text.

The single question with which we have struggled most is how to render *ignorer*. Its French meaning is, first, to not know; second, to not pay attention to; and, third, to turn away from. Although *to ignore* in English has the same meanings, the first is archaic. In translating Sartre, the temptation is to consistently render *ignorer* as *to ignore* in order to convey the "will to remain ignorant" (p. 28), and this we have done throughout the first part of the text, where the context clearly indicates this as his meaning. But beginning on page 53, when Sartre speaks about innocence, it could well be argued that his subjects, young girls, simply do not know about, for example, sex or evil, rather than actively seeking to avoid knowing about them. On the other hand, in the note to page 54, Sartre indicates that innocence is a "myth," and on page 55 that it actively applies itself to not knowing sexuality. Although it seems to us that *to ignore* is thus as defensible here as *to not know*, we have chosen the latter because of the ambiguity of the text, and we have placed the French in brackets.

On page 59, a third discussion begins that centers on *ignorer*. This stresses the fact that all knowing takes place against a background of ignorance. Here Sartre uses *ignorer* in a more neutral epistemological sense. Accordingly, except in one or two places during this discussion where Sartre clearly has intention in mind, we render *ignorer* as *to not know* and place the French in brackets.

We have placed the text pages in the exact order in which they appear in the French edition. However, a close reading suggests that pages 1–2 can best be read directly in light of the discussions of historialization and historization with which *Truth and Existence* proper ends. Sartre himself placed this title atop the manuscript page corresponding to page 3. The pages placed before this by Elkaïm-Sartre seem to us to be a note originally intended by Sartre to further develop thoughts on pages 75–80. In response to our query to this effect Elkaïm-Sartre replied as follows:

> In regard to pages 1–2. One mustn't change the order of the text, it is the order in which Sartre thought, and *Truth and Existence* remains a text whose construction was not definitive. Having said this, it may be noticed in other works (for example, the introduction to *Critique of Dialectical Reason*) that Sartre sometimes anticipates what he intends to demonstrate.

Accordingly, we leave these pages in the order she has presented them, and leave it up to the reader to decide where they fit best.

We wish to thank Hazel E. Barnes for her invaluable advice; Yvette Bulmer, Karen Murphy, and Christine Dagenais of the University of Windsor French Department for preparing the manuscript; and Wayne State University for financial assistance.

Ronald Aronson and Adrian van den Hoven

1. If there is such a mode of common being as inauthenticity, then all of History is inauthentic and action in History results in inauthenticity; authenticity reverts to individualism. Conversely, if the nature of man is to be realized at the end of History, inauthenticity must be willed for itself as the very condition of historical struggle. Any doctrine of conversion runs the real risk of being an a-historicism.[1] Any doctrine of historicity runs the real risk of being an amoralism.[2]

2. To be or to historialize ourselves? If it is *to be*, History is inessential. But History itself, if it has a meaning, makes itself in order that man *may be* (progress, dialectics, etc. . . .). History's adventurer historializes himself *for History* (in order that the historical process may come about through him, in order to be a historical agent). Thus the goal is indifferent.[3] Another aspect of the inessentiality of the goal: destiny. Spengler. Man historializes himself within the perspective of the acceptance of a destiny; he historializes himself either by accepting that the historical process is what it must be and by cooperating with it—or by accepting that his historical position is futile (tragic position). In any case the objective falls outside the human will. Historical pleasure is posited for itself. To enjoy destiny. On the other hand, if the goal is essential, History is only a means; it is inessential-essential. For example, for Marx it will be *prehistory*. We must then reject all historical complacency while knowing that we cannot enjoy Being. As for this Being itself, it is conceived in the inau-

thentic (happiness or the harmonious society), because it is first of all posited by needs (hunger, revolt against slavery, etc.).

a) Man must seek Being, but through historialization. His lot is historialization towards *Being*. Being is the *idea*. Lived experience [*le vécu*], the domain of ethics, this is History for Being.

b) Authenticity must be sought in historialization.[4] The end of History is the myth which perpetually penetrates History and gives it a meaning. But History perpetually postpones this end.[5]

To consider that the unknowable and the unverifiable fall outside of man: this is positivism. Man is a being without relationship to what he cannot know. Man is defined by what he *can* know. The antithesis: to define man by mystery—the mystical position.[6] At night all cows are gray. (1) Reject the notion of mystery. (2) Reject the fact that man defines himself solely through forms of knowledge and ignorance which are only the absence of possible forms of knowledge. Certainly *questioning* comes into the universe through man. But as soon as the world is illuminated through the general category of questioning, questions begin to form. In a universe *in question*, to know if the planets are inhabited is an objective question. Man is the being through whom questions come into the world; but man also is the being to whom questions come into the world that concern him and that he cannot resolve. Thus man defines himself in relationship to an original ignorance. He possesses a profound relationship to this ignorance. He defines what he is and what he seeks in terms of it.

TRUTH AND EXISTENCE

The only kind of unconditioned existence: Hegel's absolute-subject.* The In-itself collapses if it does not become For-itself. Unfortunately there are *consciousnesses* and there is being-in-itself. What remains of this *absolute-subject* for the individual consciousness? First of all, that it is *an* absolute subject. Because it is first of all *for-itself.* But it is only (absolute) for-itself to the extent that it is consciousness of the In-itself. And the In-itself will never be In-itself for itself but In-itself for a consciousness that is not it. Then *knowledge* appears. The In-itself-For-itself is a pure type of *being.* Thus

---

*What makes us believe that the truth identifies itself with Being, is that indeed all that exists for human-reality exists in the form of truth (these trees, these tables, these windows, these books that surround me are truths) because all that has already appeared to man exists in the form of "there is." *The world is true.* I live amid the true and the false. The beings that manifest themselves to me are given as true and subsequently they sometimes reveal themselves as false. The For-itself lives in the truth like a fish in the water.

We say that error is *appearance.* This is false. On the contrary, appearance is *always true* if we confine ourselves to it. Appearance is being. That tree that I take for a man is not a man in appearance and a tree in reality. In *appearance* (that is to say as immediate apparition) it is this somewhat darker thing that surged up in the night. And *this is true:* it is the surging up of a being. And it is my verifiable anticipation that is false to the extent that it aims at the deeper reality. In other words, in the couple of appearance and reality (a false couple invented for the sake of the argument) the appearance is always true and the error resides at the level of reality. The appearance *is* always revelation of being, reality *can* be or not be revelation of being.

3

consciousness is not knowledge but existence (see *Being and Nothingness*).[7]

The doubling of Being is necessary to Being. Besides, this doubling results in the modification of its presence-to-itself. The absolute-subject is nonsubstantial. But in relation to the In-itself of which it is consciousness, consciousness *cannot be* that of which it is conscious. The latter is tied to being only insofar as it exists for an absolute subject. Thus the known-being is a hybrid and incomplete being. It is a being for itself which does not attain unconditioned being and which becomes being for *one* absolute subject. The subject is absolute but is *nothing* but the consciousness of the In-itself; the In-itself is something but it can only be maintained in its being through the absolute-subject which it is not. Thus *to know*, is to draw Being from the night of Being without being able to lead it to the translucency of the For-itself. In spite of everything, to know is to confer a dimension of being onto Being: luminosity.

Truth is therefore a certain dimension that comes to Being through consciousness. Truth is the being-as-it-is of a being for an absolute-subject. At the level of the *cogito* it becomes useless to speak of truth because we have only *being* (existence). The essence of truth is the "there is" [*il y a*] of "there is being." The love of truth is the love of Being and the love of Being's function making Being present [*présentification de l'Etre*].[8] Seeking truth would not be so fascinating if it were only a question of determining what Being is totally without any relationship to me. Nor would this be the case, if truth were creation. But truth is Being as it is, to the extent that I confer on it a new dimension of being. Being is the night. To be illuminated already means to be something else. In illuminating, the absolute-subject goes right up to the point at which it would justify its existence by recovering the In-itself and by making it an In-itself and For-itself.* But it is stopped

---

*Beginning of the exposition

Heidegger writes: A behavior letting Being be as it is.[9] This is the starting point.

by Nothing, the insurmountable limit of not-being. Yet it has a relationship of being with the In-itself since it exists in order that *there may be* an In-itself. The revelation of the In-itself as pure event, happening to the In-itself as a new virtual dimension of being of the In-itself, this is the absolute-subject. Thus truth is an absolute event whose appearance coincides with the upsurge of human-reality and History.

Truth begins as a history of Being and it *is* a history of Being, since it is progressive disclosure of Being. Truth disappears with man. Being then sinks back into timeless night. Thus truth is the temporalization of Being such as it is insofar as the absolute-subject confers on it a progressive unveiling as a new dimension of being. It goes without saying that truth is total because the absolute-subject is totalizing. By its appearance in Being it makes there be a totality of Being. This concrete totality of Being is Truth, since it is what is revealed. Thus truth is not a logical and universal organization of abstract "truths": it is the totality of Being to the extent that it is manifested as a *there is* in the historialization of human-reality. Yet truth cannot be for just *a single* absolute-subject. If I communicate a revealed manifestation, I commu-

---

Two attitudes towards truth:

1. Truth = passivity. Contemplation of Being as it is. We insist on the presence of Being (which I cannot alter).

2. Truth = activity. Construction of the true as the first system of representations. (We insist on the construction-subjectivity. We must *act* to understand.)

Heidegger's sentence provides the synthesis: to construct *in order* to leave the subject unaltered. To construct in order to reveal the unconstructed. *To behave* in order to let Being develop itself in its untouched reality as if it were *alone*. To create what is.

The initial problem is *therefore:*

What is the kind of behavior that can be creative of the already-being and that can create it through a series of acts as it is in its uncreated nature?

Then what is consciousness and what is Being for this behavior to be possible?

And if knowledge bases itself on immediate contact or intuition, then what is an intuition that is not contemplative (passive) without being Husserl's constitutive intuition?

5

nicate it with my revealing behavior, with the outline and selection that I performed on it; *with contours*. In this case, what is given to the other is an in-itself-for-itself. If I say the table is round, I communicate to the other an already unveiled and already cut-out object in the totality of objects, exactly as if I handed him a penholder (*already worked* wood). At this moment, the In-itself appears to the newcomer as For-itself, as subjectivity. It is In-itself and it is also what a subjectivity reveals of the In-itself (I judge my companion by what he shows me of the landscape). At the same time the For-itself becomes In-itself: by transcending the *vision* and the *statement* towards my own ends, I make an object of them on my path and a *truth* precisely in the sense that truth is the objectivity of the subjective: Galileo's *insight* [*la vue*] becomes law.

If Peter points out the table to me, I see it *through* Peter's consciousness. At this point the new absolute-subject integrates the universe into the human. Indeed the object is no longer to be unveiled as in-itself but is to be rendered present [*apprésenter*][10] as *already unveiled*, that is to say that I recover the unveiled. This unveiling becomes the basis in itself on which the object *is* form as subjective. What I see of the object, is the already-seen by another who has-not-gone-farther in the unveiling. If *I go farther*, the discovered totality is subjective (it is the subjective finitude which appears to me and which is my starting point). At this moment the already-known, insofar as it is *only* this limited unveiling, is an in-itself (object, law) that I recover in the for-itself by transcending it towards a new unveiling.

Thus the absolute-subject who discovers truth must want to discover it *for others* in order that it may pass through a stage of *in-itself* and then be recovered as *for-itself*. By itself alone, it can only live, be [*exister*] its disclosing behavior as for-itself and on the level of certainty. It cannot manifest it to itself on the level of the in-itself to be revealed, that is, on the level of *truth*. But if he *makes a gift of it*, the disclosure enters the rank of signifying object, of indicating object, and it is then recovered by the sole fact that the indication becomes

6

for the other an instrument that becomes one with his own behavior.

Thus judgment is an interindividual phenomenon. *I* do not need to judge: I *see*. I judge only for the other. Judgment is an indicative gesture to the other, both objective and subjective but for the other (that is to say in-itself and for-itself). But I live reciprocally in the *Mitsein* and I see only to indicate to the other. Or rather, often I see only by indicating. Thus man sees for the other, or sees the already seen. Thus is consolidated the new dimension of the In-itself that came out of the night revealed by an absolute-subject, and whose unveiling in turn exists for another absolute-subject that grasps it first as In-itself, then recovers it. This is what we call *Truth*. It is the In-itself as it has appeared to a for-itself when its appearance, as subjective, unveils itself to another for-itself as in-itself. And in turn, for me as absolute subject who was the first to *unveil*, my unveiling, which was purely lived, is given back to me as absolute-object by the other if first of all *I give it to him*. I am then in-itself for myself insofar as one returns the lived unveiling to me as known truth. But if I realize anew the unveiling intuition, I recover the in-itself-truth and my truth becomes for me in itself and for itself. Thus the total truth is a concrete reality because it is the development of the manifestation across *all* human history and the manifestation is manifestation of *everything*. Yet the ideal of Truth is not the recovery of the entire object by subjectivity conceived as totality. For the In-itself, in manifesting itself, remains In-itself and will never dissolve itself in any for-itself. Besides, the unveiling subjectivity will always require a subjectivity that transforms its unveiling into in-itself for-itself because mankind is a detotalized-totality. The ideal of Truth is only that *all* of Being be illuminated and that it remain so.

On the other hand, it must be understood that *truth* is a kind of recovery of the In-itself by itself. This is because Being always reveals itself to a point of view and we are tempted to turn this point of view into subjectivity. But this is not so. Subjectivity is only *the illumination*. In fact, the point of view defines itself *objectively* in worldly terms. The penholder appears as it must appear to a being situated in the midst of the world who is defined by the functioning of a retina according to the physical laws of optics. The error of sensationalism is due precisely to believing that the phenomenon of perception obeys objective laws since the point of view defines itself objectively. Therefore perception does not permit us to get out of the world except insofar as it is perception.* But it is already a roughly outlined doubling of the In-itself since the point of view is totally definable as In-itself (as the neo-realists have already remarked). And outside of this, *nothing* except the illumination of the whole system. It is therefore Being appearing to Being. But *appearance* is non-being and subjectivity; here is a circle that cannot be completed.

Yet this incomplete doubling assures truth of its *reality* character. The In-itself does not appear before a transmundane being that would be in a state of indifferent exteriority in relation to it. The world appears to a being in the midst of the world: the conditions of appearance of the In-itself are defined by the In-itself. Thus perception is interiorization of the world, and, in a sense, presence of the world to itself. When I touch velvet, what I make exist is neither a velvet that is absolute and in itself nor a velvet relative to some sort of structure superimposed [*structure de survol*] by a transmundane consciousness. I make *velvet* exist *for flesh*. Food is manifested in the world as food to a being in the midst of the world. Therefore it is an absolute quality. The reality therefore is that the being that manifests truth is in the world, is of the world, and is in danger in the world. The reality is that the illuminator can be destroyed (or strengthened or overcome) by what it illuminates. This belonging to the world of truth, or Reality, can also be defined as the fact that truth is *experienced* or lived. In a sense, all truth is lived as danger, effort, risk (even a "scientific" truth) and, conversely, all that is lived (in rage, fear, shame, love, flight, good or bad faith), manifests Truth.

*A long time ago we got rid of our grandfathers' ghosts. We should now get rid of our great-grandchildren's ghosts.[11]

8

The Truth cannot remain the property of the unique absolute-subject. It is in order to be given. The absolute-subject transmits what it sees as one transmits names and powers (in matronymics). The Truth is a *gift*. But if this gift refers us back to the infinite, Truth is *in danger*. Indeed, if I consider the ideal demands of Truth, a harmonious end of History is required, that is to say a crowning of subjectivity, an ultimate subjectivity which gives its meaning to Truth, which concludes. Then Truth is no longer *in order to be given*, its ultimate meaning is stable and egoistic contemplation: we are the means for which that final consciousness is the end. And the meaning of Truth is no longer to be a gift that is lived, but contemplation. And this all-knowing genera- tion[12] rediscovers a superimposed transcendence in relation- ship to the world.* It faces the unitary collection of knowable and manipulable objects. We return to the old theory of the contemplation of the world by a being that surveys it from on high.

Besides, if History has an end, it vanishes because the means becomes the inessential and the end the essential; temporality is denied. Even the Hegelian (and true) concep- tion of truth having become hides a Truth that is static, be- cause if truth has to have become, that "having become" is *in the end* only a static quality of truth, just as the fact that having lived or loved a lot is a static quality of an old man. And so History has meaning as History only if its end is cata- strophic. Its internal *tragic* conflict is that it sets a limit while it will only have an end. Or, rather, the end of History is postulated as an internal limit when it is an external limit. On the other hand, it is part of the very conception of plural consciousness that *in no way* can totalization occur because plurality can not be overcome. Therefore, whatever the end of History may be, it is catastrophic for science since Truth will not be *decided*. That is, if we suppose at this very moment a destruction of the world by the atomic bomb, it will never be decided whether Marxism was true or not as an interpretation

*The last world behind the scenes is the world after tomorrow.

9

of History, what the true place is in the scientific world of the theories of Heisenberg, de Broglie, and of Einstein, nor what is the correct theory of evolution and who was right, Mendel or Lysenko. And since today's science reinserts yesterday's truths in their true place, even Greek science, even Archimedes' law is questioned, if not as bald statement at least as meaning.

But by discovering the finitude of History philosophy has liberated us, because the measure of truth is now determined by a decisive act of the one who manifests it.[13] Just as a concrete gift, a present, is not anonymous but implies necessarily an *address*, similarly Truth, to the extent that it is a gift, is not anonymous. It is *my* friend, *my* wife, to whom I call to point out this or that spectacle, this or that appearance. And this is how I decide the extent of this truth: in this case I do not think at all of extending it to the cyclist who is passing by on the road. In the total historialization of the for-itself, which assumes a lived knowledge of its place in relationship to yesterday, today, and tomorrow and defines this place as an absolute, there is *the choice* of the consciousnesses to whom this truth is given in order that they may live it: this is the concrete universal of today and tomorrow. By defining my power I leave in the dark the infinitude that will follow or, rather, I still hand them my truth but as freedoms exterior to my history; these freedoms will reassume it to make of it whatever they want. In a sense, I define *our* "end of history" within a larger history; by choosing a finished history, I interiorize the limit of History. It should be understood that this is how a future is defined.

"We Write for Our Own Time"[14] has been understood to mean writing for our *present*. But no, it is writing for a concrete future defined by each and everyone's hopes, fears and possibilities of action. These fifty, these hundred years suffice to define the region of truth in which I move. Truth is subjective. The truth of an age is its meaning, its climate, etc., to the extent that they are lived as discovery of Being. Spengler is right from the point of view of subjectivity: each age lives and dies. Marx is right from the point of view of objectivity: the age dies without dying, without our being able to fix the date of its death; it is assumed, overcome, analyzed; its truths, by changing meaning, are integrated, and moreover everyone determines his living past as well as his living future. But both are wrong to the extent that they play on objectivity-subjectivity. According to Spengler the subjective finitude of the age *makes itself* until death, and he lets us slide into the objective under the name of destiny. But it is the next generation that decides that the age has had such or such a destiny, because it is dead. According to Marx the present age determines the objective for the previous age. And so for each generation. But because of the fact that there is a tradition of the objective, we want to suppress the element of subjectivity which is the environment of objectivity. Objectivity is broken, it sustains itself in the element of the subjective which is perpetually surging up, and we want to make it the framework and the continuous principle of all subjectivity.

This does not mean at all that the truth I defend appears to me relative *to my age*; this has no meaning at all.* It is true for me in the absolute and I give it to others as absolute. And

---

*For the individual person there are also living and dead truths. A truth is dead when verified and consecrated by the other, and when we no longer enter into it and it can no longer be verified again in a circular manner. Truth then becomes an in-itself (because it has been congealed into in-itself by the other). It is a thing in the world, a set character trait (I am he who has said that . . .) or *property* of him who has discovered it. (I have always said it, etc.)

From this point of view it is easy to understand what an *idea* is. An idea is *always* the project of deciphering an in-itself in the light of an end. The end is not *idea* but only grasping of the these as means. Thus an idea is always *practical*. (In pure knowledge, it is practical because it is a verifying schema. A mathematical *idea* is the outline of the operations that provide the solution.) From the point of view of its formal (subjective) reality an idea is a future conduct [*une conduite à venir*] towards Being, which comes to me through Being. An idea is the mathematization of possibles. From the objective point of view (objective reality), it has the *intended* [visé] being-in-itself that it borrows from Being. It is *the future of Being* that comes to Being, that is, the intending of a new state of Being. It is myself as possible presence for a new state of Being. The operational schema is the consciousness (of) *doing* (non-thetic consciousness) and the consciousness of the object is consciousness of the obtained-Being in correlation with the operation. I am before the *present* in-itself in the posture of an *outline of a behavior*. This behavior,

11

it is indeed absolute. Simply, I determine the period when it will be alive. It will be alive as long as it is illumination, revelation, commitment for the other: this was the case with the earth's rotation in Galileo's time, with the circulation of blood in Harvey's time, with gravitation in Newton's time. In that particular period one *wills* it: to judge is to will, to risk oneself, to commit our lives to the revelation. It passes to the next generations and dies. This does not mean that it loses its exactness but that it becomes a pure instrument or self-evident a priori structure of facts. The idea, as illumination of the In-itself through a subjectivity, becomes law.

To the following generations the law becomes fact. ("It is a *fact*" that the earth rotates.) It is dead. An eternal truth is a dead truth that has returned to the In-itself. A truth has not *become*, it is *becoming* [devenante]. And at the end of its becoming, it dies. That does not mean that it becomes false. It becomes *indeterminate*, that is, we no longer grasp it in its context and with its articulations but as a bone with which

---

being contact with Being, is *in-itself* and completely an outline in Being of a future of Being. This future is and is not in Being. If I raise up this block in order to place it on the slope, I constitute the slope as future to the block and the block as future pressure on the slope. Block and slope are, and I move from one to the other in order to constitute that borrowed being which is the slope (that I see) *for* the being (the stone) that I carry, being that I carry for the slope (that I see). This back-and-forth movement produces the borrowed being, the future in-itself of the in-itself, or the objective reality of the operational schema.

The second stage of the idea is its living verification, the moment when behavior absorbs itself in the object, when it metamorphoses itself by and through the object into *a characteristic in itself* of the object or *result* of the operation. Either the trait is inscribed in the object by my knife (and it surges up under my sight as a momentarily indestructible form) or it is unveiled by my sight as already inscribed (in both cases the verifying movement is the same; but in the first the vision is at the tip of the knife). At that moment, as we have seen, the objective and the subjective are complementary: I have created what is.

Third stage of the idea: it is *stated* for the other. The other makes of the statement an in-itself. He gives me back the idea in the form of in-itself (perpetual indicator of the object). At that moment the idea is dead. It is a thing, as long as I do not slip myself into it by recovering it.

one constitutes a new organism. At that moment it is altogether a matter of indifference to know *how* it has become:
Archimedes' law, in becoming dead, no longer interests anyone. But since man has for a long time linked himself with
the Eternal, he has preferred dead truths to living truths and
he has created a theory of Truth which is a theory of death.

The foundation of Truth is freedom. Thus man can choose
non-truth. This non-truth is ignorance or lie. On the other
hand, unveiling implies that what is unveiled is originally
veiled. Subjectively, this means that man's condition is originally ignorance. Finally the unveiling behavior is activity: to
allow Being to appear as it is, we have to go and look for it.
Thus error. These are the different points we must examine.

Everything starts with sight [*vue*] and ends with sight (intuition). But sight conceived as pure contemplative repose
can neither reveal the how of an object nor its multiple facets.
It would already be—if it could exist as absolute passivity in repose—a relationship to *something*, simply because
consciousness cannot exist without being conscious of grasping a something (ontological argument in *Being and Nothingness*).[15] But this something would be pure nonqualified
presence. Simple permanence, identity or nonalteration of
presence, therefore supposes already that consciousness lasts
in the face of the permanent. And duration, if it is not itself a
behavior, is the foundation of all behaviors. Thus pure consciousness—if we could conceive of it—*exists* as revelatory
of *Being* but not of any manner of being. However varied the
object may be, the very notion of variety can only be acquired
through a unifying behavior. Indeed, pure consciousness defines itself as internal negation of Being (I demonstrated this
in *Being and Nothingness*).[16]

But this negation, if it did not choose itself immediately,
would only be existence without qualification as negation of
nonparticularized Being-in-itself. In truth, this relationship—
conceived here through pure abstraction—would be quite
fundamental, in the sense that the upsurge of consciousness
near Being would be revelatory of Being-in-itself as being of
any phenomenon. And this being would not at all be the phe-

nomenon of being nor would it be the being of a particular being, but it would be the concrete being of the In-itself (neither of several, nor of one, nor of all of the In-itself, since these are subsequent qualifications). Therefore Being is present in an undifferentiated manner to consciousness. But this is the case to the exact extent that, right into this supposedly immobile upsurge, consciousness is act (it makes itself what it is). It is so to the extent that human-reality has another dimension than the present, it is so to the extent that it must come to itself as project, that Being unveils itself to it. In sum, knowledge exists on the ground of anticipation. Any project unveils, all unveiling results from a project.* But here we are not dealing with a pure succession of moments each one of which would contribute a *given* which would only be undifferentiated presence of Being. The In-itself reveals itself to a being that throws itself towards the future and that determines its manner of being; in short, truth reveals itself to action. All action is knowledge (even though in most cases it is a manner of nonintellectual unveiling) and all knowledge,

---

Language: the essential of the *sign:* to lend its *being* to the project which, otherwise, would be pure subjectivity.

Principle: the subjective, or presence to itself or nihilation of Being, can in no way *produce* being. Any project, be it invention, unveiling or word, that concerns Being and consequently has an objective reality (intended by Being) must necessarily borrow from Being that future being it intends. What *is not there* (the absent Peter, my far-away home) cannot be conceived, imagined or named by me, if it is not through a being that lends me its being. I have to surpass that being towards the absent being. Two ways: sign or image.

The idea is never *subjective* except in the sense that it is future, as nonthetic consciousness to *my* present non-thetic consciousness. This only means that it exists according to the structural mode of all truth (in-itself for a for-itself). It is always to come from Being-in-itself *for* Being-in-itself. An idea is *always* the unity of a result in Being and of the modifications of Being that will lead to it. The indissoluble unity of a theorem and of the mathematical construction which demonstrates it (that *makes* it be *seen*), a law of physics (structure of Being) and the test that verifies it, or *conversely* of a *new state of Being* (transformation into instrument) and *visions* that permit us to find the means to obtain it (truth being here a *stage* of the construction). Example: the construction of this float implies *the truth* of Archimedes' law.

even intellectual knowledge, is action. Because the *Nur ver-weilen bei*[17] of science is not passive contemplation.

It is a refusal to use the object *practically*, but not a refusal of anticipation. The physicist constructs his hypothesis and his experimental apparatus. We *see* nothing that we have not first of all *foreseen*. But, precisely, this foresight and this anticipation cannot themselves be pure givens: they cannot come to us from the depth of our memory, evoked by the purely mechanical link of associations. They could not even come to us from the depth of the future, sent or emitted as particles of the future by some God, because we would then be constrained to decipher them by means of new hypotheses. The "contents" of consciousness would precisely be in-itselves that we would have to define by anticipation or leave in a state of pure undifferentiated presences. We would gain nothing by this. Obviously we have to be our own hypothesis, that is, we have to exist as an anticipatory and revelatory behavior of the object that is being considered. This is what Husserl understood by "empty intentions" awaiting a missing intuition. But his theory of time did not allow him to see that these empty intentions straddled the present in order to be its future. We are replacing the empty intention by *the project of discovery*. The richness of a for-itself is measured by the multiplicity of its projects, and these constitute exactly the quantity of being that is given to it to reveal.

Obviously, therefore, the foundation of all revelation of

Conversely, the *truth* of Archimedes' law implies its verification through the construction of a float. The useful envelops the true, the true envelops the useful. The idea is never purely practical nor purely theoretical: it is practico-theoretical or theoretico-practical.

The idea is not a judgment or a virtual unification changing nothing in the object: it is the project of a real unification. There are no a priori synthetic judgments because they are not needed since there is no ontological permanence of knowledge. There is freedom as foundation of *real* syntheses to be made. Through man synthesis enters into the universe. And he unveils it by effecting it. The placing in relationship comes from the fact that man is relationship to self through Being. And this establishment of the relationship is always *operational*. It inscribes itself in Being.

being is freedom, that is, the mode of being of a being that is to itself its own project. There can be knowledge only to the extent that there is freedom. A Kantian and atemporal freedom could not replace our notion of freedom temporalizing itself, because if it remains outside the phenomenal universe, the pure synthetic work of a priori judgments is obscure to itself and has its reason outside of it. But, at the same time, the possibility of unveiling implies for the same reason the possibility of not-unveiling. Included in the very act by which I anticipate the unveiling is the possibility that I would have had to forgo it. Otherwise the unveiling would be pure necessity and therefore nonknowledge, as I have just shown. The very idea of *knowing*, of unveiling, can have meaning only for a freedom. But, conversely, it is impossible that the upsurge of a freedom not imply an unveiling comprehension of Being and the project of unveiling. In short, no freedom without truth. This does not at all contradict what we said just now about the possibility of not unveiling, because through freedom both the veil and the unveiling come to being. And free human-reality must necessarily assume its responsibilities vis-à-vis the truth. Whatever it decides, it can act only in such a way that a truth surges up on Being at the same time as it, human-reality, surges up. All it can decide is to not *discover* this truth that comes to Being through it. The identity principle is only the specification of a much more general and fundamental principle (the identity principle is regional), namely that Being is *knowable*. And this does not mean at all that Being is *rational*, that is, that it conforms to a certain number of unifying laws, but simply that, rational or irrational, it can be unveiled in its rationality or irrationality. And this is not because of Being but because of freedom which, far from slipping into a priori categories (whether or not of identity), is conscious of itself as free of any presupposition and capable of inventing any kind of hypothesis starting from a given or, rather, of allowing itself to be guided in its invention by any type of being. To use an image, freedom is not at all linked to the identity principle: it does not presuppose that a being cannot at the same time and in the same respect be itself and

16

something other than itself (besides, we could cite a hundred examples in the social and psychological realm where the identity principle has no effect, not even a regulatory one—especially when we are dealing with human-reality itself taken as totality).* But only that if such a being is in the world, it disposes a priori over the power of inventing antic-ipations that will permit *seeing* it in its nonidentical reality. Besides this is the very principle of modern mathematics: we can create a mathematical logic with any presupposition. For example, if I suppose a priori an adding operation whose result is not the same when I perform the operation from right to left or from left to right, nothing keeps me—or has kept me—from constructing a mathematics using these operations. It is enough to define them. In this sense we can say that the opposition of the rational and the irrational is transcended by the profound requirement of freedom, which is not to know Being by means of this or that a priori process, but simply that Being is knowable because it is in principle knowledge. In fact, all the "principles" of knowledge or of Reason are out-side: they are instruments invented in their time by freedom in order to anticipate a reality that is hidden or half unveiled. Similarly, the point is not to affirm that everything is know-able through understanding (that is, through analysis) or, as we say, through representation. But any behavior, because it is free and it is in the world, in the midst of Being—whether it be intellectual, practical, or affective—unveils being and makes *truths* appear.

We have just shown that truth appears only to free projects. We must now show the reverse: that all free behavior is revelatory—unveiling. The clarification of the structures of freedom makes this clear. Indeed all free behavior posits an end. But free behavior is surpassing of Being by a being situ-ated in the midst of Being. The end is *to* come to Being. It transcends it and preserves it within itself. Therefore it en-

---

*[Therefore, the affirmation that Being is knowable implies no presupposi-tion on Being but the pure consciousness that freedom has of itself. Freedom is bearing on Being, adaptation to Being.]

velops an understanding of Being, since in Being it must come to Being. At the same time, as an end, it groups the beings that are present in a meaningful unity; they become means. And, as I have already explained, the synthesis of *all* the means cannot be distinguished from the end.[18] This means that the end is the illuminating organization of means. Thus the structure of truth is necessarily that what *is* is illuminated by what is not. The veri-fying movement [*mouvement veri-fiant*] goes from the future that is not to the present that is. It is only through a being which is not yet what it is that truth can come to Being; Being is true only in and through transcendence [*dépassement*]. But this implies necessarily that truth temporalizes itself, that is, that it appears according to the categories of before and after. Indeed, since it is the project that illuminates Being, Being is obscure before the project and, to the extent that the end to come draws nearer to the present, Being illuminates itself more and more; the end modifies itself to the extent that it realizes itself, because it always complicates itself more and more, and it illuminates more and more detailed regions of being. Thus, the revealed being is correlative to the projected end: when the end is altogether summary and undifferentiated, the being revealed in the project is global and abstract; to the extent that I work at the realization, the end is detailed through being and reacts by detailing being. In the end being and the realized end are one and the same: the unveiling has been completed.

But therefore this assumes *ignorance* as the starting point from which truth slowly extricates itself. Here we are not dealing with an absolute ignorance or one of exteriority. If, for example, a specific physical phenomenon is presently occurring in a Japanese city, I am unaware of it in the sense that I have not one hint of it and consequently I am unaware of my ignorance. But this absolute ignorance, which exists when we consider only a specific fact with which I have no relationship and whose relationship with the world I do not envisage, is not the ignorance that characterizes my initial relationship with the truth. Indeed my first relationship is with the entire world, and my surging up in it is already an enterprise vis-à-vis the world. The world is the fundamental unity which appears in Being as correlative of my brute and fundamental enterprise of existing. Now the world gives itself immediately as plenitude of being and as infinitely rich and undifferentiated raw material for the infinity of my possible projects. Also, when surging up in the world, I grasp the fact that the illumination of this world is my constant possibility. This means that I grasp that the truth of the world is immediately my possibility and that my own temporalization will temporalize the truth, i.e., will illuminate more and more detailed regions of the world. Therefore, at the start *everything* is given to me in undifferentiated form, as correlative of my undifferentiated project of existing, and I have the original understanding that in my choosing myself I will choose the illumination of certain intramundane areas.

Thus, to say that I do not know originally, is to say that the truth is my possibility awaiting me and I am the being through whom the truth will come from within into the world. To say that I do not know is to say that I am aware that I can know, that is, that the world is *already* knowable. When Socrates says, "I know that I know nothing," this modesty is by the same token the most radical affirmation of man because it supposes that *everything* is *to be known*. Thus, ignorance does not derive from a denial of the world which supposedly is hiding its secrets from me. Quite the contrary, all of Being is *present* to me from the moment of my surging up, and the child's first encounter is not with abstract sensation but with the world. My ignorance derives from the fact that I can grasp what is present to me only by temporalizing myself in behaviors that aim at the future. Human-reality can receive nothing passively: it must always conquer, not by virtue of some curse but by virtue of its manner of being. It is because the child *does* nothing that it *knows* nothing, and it learns insofar as it does. The unveiling of truth has stopped for certain societies or people because they perpetually move in the same circle of tradition. It is said that they are impermeable to experience but this is not true. Because it is not experience that can change their traditions, but in changing

19

their traditions they will change their experience. We can look directly at an object and not *see* it if it is not given in a perspective that is part of behavior.

Therefore, the illumination of Being begins from Non-Being: I understand the state of France, my political party, my denominational group, in terms of what I would want it to be, in terms of what I project it to become. In other words, Non-Being intervenes directly as structure of truth or as illumination of Being. This remark is of some importance if we want to understand what error is. Indeed, since Plato it is customary to assimilate truth with Being and error with Non-Being. From this arise endless aporias, because there is such a heterogeneity between the nature of truth that *is* and of error that *is not* that it is impossible to understand how we can mistake one for the other and how, if the True, the Efficacious, and the Good define themselves as plenitude of Being, there can be a certain efficacy of error, that is, a certain being of Non-Being. But if the category of Action gives a certain primacy to Non-Being over Being and if the truth is a structure, a moment of the action, there is a certain non-being on the horizon. If truth is a certain non-being of Being, it is, at first sight, more easily understandable that there is a certain being of Non-Being or error. So Nothingness intervenes in truth at three points:

1. From the side of the In-itself as power of making the Being collapse which is not for-itself, that is, the Night of Being.

2. From the side of the For-itself, as the illumination of Being by Non-Being, which implies that Being appears always in suspense in the heart of what is not. The *provisional* nature of all truth; which also implies the necessity of temporalization and, consequently, that illumination appears necessarily on a ground of ignorance, since each one of my projects appears on the undifferentiated ground of possibles that I do not possibilize.

3. From the side of the relationship of the For-itself and the In-itself. Because a gulf of nothingness prevents the In-

itself from becoming For-itself and prevents the For-itself from reabsorbing into itself and recovering the In-itself.

Error would be impossible for the In-itself-for-itself: it is impossible in Hegel and Spinoza. But it is precisely here that we discover the *Not-being* [*Ne-pas-être*], since the In-itself *is not* the For-itself. If truth is this complex game of Being and Not-being, we can better understand that complex game of Not-being and Being that is error.

The In-itself is illuminated by an anticipation. But whatever this anticipation may be, its objective essence is to intend the In-itself and it can only aim at the In-itself (being subjective intention as far as its formal reality is concerned) because the In-itself *is*. In other words, there are only two realities about which I cannot make a mistake: the modes of the For-itself that I am and the presence of the In-itself. I can be entirely mistaken, take a tree for a boundary marker, think in the night that there is "someone there" when there is no one; at least the tree is there, the night is there. In short, there is always something that is in-itself and whose initial unveiling is contemporaneous with my own surging up: Being is self-evident. And if the In-itself were not, I would not even be able to conceive it since I am pure for-itself. Yet I anticipate the In-itself that invades me, I transcend it towards an end which is *my* end. But this end is in the world and it commands anticipations about the In-itself that have an objective reality, i. e., which are anticipations of the manner of being of the In-itself.

For example, that "something" is *a tree*. This *tree* which is as yet *not-seen*, which precedes sight and constructs it, is, as *tree*, a non-being. It has *existence* only as my own subjectivity (circuit of selfness) which comes to me from the depths of the future. But as non-being it is not *nothing*. It is a *something* that is not me and that is not yet. It draws its being from the being-in-itself that it anticipates. Anticipation transcends the revealed being towards the future and retains its *being* from that being; it has a borrowed being exactly like consciousness. But it is the opposite: it is as for-itself, as presence

21

to itself, that consciousness is supported by the In-itself, and it is as intention of in-itself that the In-itself supports the anticipation: The latter thus functions as a measure and guiding schema of *vision*. Because, as we have already stated, vision is not passive contemplation, it is an operation. Persuaded that that *something* is a tree, I generate the tree on that *something*, just as Kant insists that to perceive a line is to draw it. This means that I mime the vision of the tree, I retain each element of the vision in an organization called *tree*. I create what is. If the in-itself *allows itself to be seen* as tree, it organizes itself within my view in such a way that it answers the questions that my eye asks of it, so that my attempt to "see" this obscure mass "as branches" is crowned with success and suddenly a *form* constitutes itself that I can no longer undo. For this reason, after finding the hat in the drawing, I can see nothing but the hat. Thus the form that has surged up in my operation suddenly raises itself up *against me* as indestructible.

But at the same time, if I can not undo it, I can realize indefinitely the generating operation and therefore I am both creative and passive. This is the appearance of truth, or Being appearing in the act. From the subjective point of view, knowledge does not differ from creation and, conversely, creation is knowledge; we have a moment of knowledge. But, at the same time, the congealed appearance of Being is autonomous, independent; it is an answer. If, on the contrary, Being is a dense refusal of being "seen as a tree," anticipation annihilates itself. Indeed it can only continue to be sustained by subjectivity, but subjectivity cannot sustain it as a mortgage on the objective, as objective intention. From this point of view it is nothingness or simple subjective memory of having been. Obviously the object answers to demands (if it does not answer them, its nonanswer is an answer: it indicates provisional indetermination, because the object is not in the present field of our action), but it answers only *to demands*. Thus, little by little, the project complicates itself, the end comes closer and specifies itself, the questions multiply themselves as the *vision* or intuitions multiply themselves. The totality of the object's verified answers constitutes its truth: its truth, of course, *in the light of that project*. Other projects would allow other truths to rise up unified with the first ones since the object delivers no truths other than those that are asked of it (of course, sometimes the answer overflows the question, but this is within a framework of previously defined investigations; and besides, in this case, the answer is rather the indication of new questions to be posed).

In a sense, therefore, there is no error; anticipation is a non-being which gets its being from the anticipated in-itself. It is, in order to be verified, it annihilates itself if it does not allow a correct construction.* And as the realization of an end is pursued through verifying behavior, the limit of verification is the realization of the end. "The truth of the pudding," said James, "is in the eating." The verification of the salt in the salt shaker is that I salt my meat and that it has a salty taste when I eat it. If it has a sweet taste it is because it was sugar. To be truthful we can choose to say that I made *a mistake*, but this is because the verification takes place at my expense. In reality we are dealing only with a negative verification annihilating my anticipations.

We call errors catastrophic verifications, but this is from the utilitarian point of view. We may prefer less costly verifications but they win out only in economy and in usefulness. However, since verification is always in process, the In-itself is surrounded by not yet verified anticipations which get their being from it and their character *to come* [à-venir], from me. Thus we can equally consider them as a present characteristic (but only as probable or possible) of this particular in-itself, or as a project of future verification. Therefore, the (hidden) base of that saucer is just as much the present of being as it is the future goal of my gesture.

Therefore, present being is non-being *to* come [à venir]. A non-being of Being surrounds it on every side. In particular,

---

*[My pencil drops. I pick it up. What proves that it is the same pencil? The fact that I pick it up (Bergson, preface to *Pragmatism*).[19] No. But coherence of the *action* implying permanence (Merleau-Ponty).]

once the anticipation has been verified it can just as easily return to its nature as anticipation. I have turned over the saucer, there has been verification and intuition. I put it down again, its base is hidden from me, the existence of the base is again anticipation. But this time we call it knowledge because it relates to a vision that has already been accomplished. It remains nevertheless a non-being, drawing its being from the specific in-itself; but for reasons derived from the nature of objects, from their inertia, from my previous experiences, I decide to integrate it into my very perception of the object. This means that I perceive this ground verywhere *through* my real vision, that is everywhere *through the object* and, conversely, that I interpret the object in terms of that ground.* This time there is affirmation. Not at all in my judgment but in my very perception. This affirmation is still an operation: I construct my vision on new anticipations and starting from the solid ground of the old one.

This affirmation is freedom: I could just as well doubt. But to doubt is not to act; it is also to project an end in the future, since it is an undertaking. I decide to act, that is, to *risk*. At this level, truth becomes risk, meaning that *there is a non-being of Being* (it depends, in its manifest being, on a verification that is to come and that is considered as having occurred, or, rather, there is a whole important dimension of its present being which *is not* given in intuition and yet which is present in its very character as absence). There is also a being of Non-Being (the aspect of the saucer that is present lends its being to the invisible one; the invisible one which is not or is *perhaps* not, figures, as being, in vision itself, throws its weight

---

*Since man's position vis-à-vis Being implies that Being is discoverable only by means of anticipation, any illumination of Being occurs through anticipation and on condition of future verification. Therefore, atomic theory is illuminating anticipation of what is revealed and will remain so for a long time, because it is a radical act of anticipation indicating an infinitely verifiable fulfilling and not a determined and immediately visible object. True or false, the atom is also non-being illuminating the infinite series of Being through its borrowed being.

in the totalisation, and confers its nature on the object). And it is precisely the non-being of Being that gives its being to Non-Being or, rather, the non-being of Being is precisely the being of Non-Being.

But this being of Non-Being is precisely the being of error. Indeed, in error, Being *is not* what we say it is, and what we say of it, which is, consequently, a non-being, still has a certain being because we can believe in it and affirm it. From this moment on, we will have to deal with a truth or error through a destiny external to the true-object. I salted my meat just now. Therefore I see the container on my right as a salt shaker. If someone, taking advantage of my not paying attention, has replaced the salt with sugar, the structure of my verifying behavior is not modified. We are still dealing with a being which sustains a non-being, truth has transformed itself into error without changing in nature. In short, as soon as we go beyond the framework of pure verifying vision, truth is the risk of error. But we *always* transcend the framework of verifying vision because verification is successive. And it is not successive by chance but because truth must temporalize itself.

Thus error is a permanent risk of a verification that is arrested or not started again. If I stop myself during the verification, it no longer depends on me that the object, grasped to the point at which I stop myself, is true or false. Verification must be a circular and continuous process. But like verification of the object, it is the use I make of it for my ends, because the verification is circular and continues as long as the use lasts. I *use* the saucer, therefore I return to the beginning of my knowledge, which again becomes anticipation and which invalidates or verifies itself in every case. Truth *in motion* is not susceptible to error; anticipations are not stopped in truth, their non-being is temporary, they are pure operational schemas for perception. Error is a stopping, a prolonged instant, passivity, and as is the case for all passivity it allows itself to be conditioned from the outside. If the verification is suspended, it is pure chance that will decide whether or not there is salt in the salt shaker, while instead continuous use of

the salt shaker during the meal amounts to an absolute verification, even though each moment taken separately represents a risk in the total process. And from this we can also
conclude that any error is *temporary* if only the object remains in an instrumental relationship with human subjectivity, because sooner or later the process of verification will
begin again—or otherwise the object falls into Nothingness
and error into forgetfulness.

Obviously error is necessary to truth because it makes
truth *possible*. Without the possibility of error, truth would
be necessary. But then it would no longer be truth, because it
implies a freely constructed vision by means of an anticipating
behavior. The possibility of error makes truth a possibility.
Error comes from outside of human-reality as a consequence
of a decision to stop the process of verification or to not start
it again. But it is fitting that human-reality not halt the verifying process. In this case the false anticipations will not
appear as errors but as simple attempts which cancel themselves out and are necessary conditions for the construction
of the vision.

It is therefore possible to consider the history of man as the
history of his errors, if we adopt the point of view of the inter-
ruptions in verification due to death, the succession of generations, violence, etc.* Just as we can also see it as an immense
verification in progress, if we note the temporary character of
each stop and the resumption of verification immediately
thereafter, as well as the circularity of the verifications in
practice (boats verifying Archimedes' law a thousand times
a day, at each moment of the day and night).

But here as elsewhere, plurality, or the existence of a detotalized totality, makes the error substantive—if, in the process of verification, I make a *gift* to the other of my arrested
truth (or error). Indeed if it is true that the unveiling of Being
by an absolute-subject is in-itself for the other and finally becomes *fact* (the earth rotates), the same process renews itself

* There are dead errors just as there are dead truths.

26

if the *gift* is the gift of an error. Error becomes *fact*, a property of humanity. But, in the depth of its substance, the fact is *false*. And as long as the resumption of verification is stopped by rituals and traditions, it will remain false, that is, affected in its core by an internal fragility.

And the same construction can be error from certain perspectives and pure moment of verification in progress from certain other perspectives. Error for those who, without going farther, adopt it as a pure, incontrovertible legacy of tradition, and verification in progress for those who seek to go farther. For many Christians in the Middle Ages, Christian ideology is pure error; for the heretics who attempt to affirm through it the right of criticism and free thought, it is verification. As an attempt to rationalize an unacceptable myth, the Arian heresy is in the movement of verification. The opponents who continue to believe what is unacceptable in the myth are in error, even if both points of view are equally removed from reality.

Thus, through the upsurge of a freedom in the heart of Being, ignorance and knowledge, error and truth appear as conjoint possibilities. But since the truth is illumination through an act and the act is choice, I must decide the truth and want it; therefore I am able to *not* want it. The condition of there being truth is the perpetual possibility of refusing it. This is how man's freedom illuminates itself: indeed everything that *appears* through him, appears through temporalization on a ground where this manifestation did not exist before. But it would be an error to regard that prior ground as Being as such, before the intervention of man, since temporalization itself rises up with man, and the before is human. Thus the ground which is the before, *without* Truth, Goodness, etc., comes into the world through man. But it immediately determines itself in its content as *before* the manifestation (before Goodness, the Result, the True) and not as an indifferent negativity. Therefore it is ordered by the future itself in its internal structure. And, conversely, it makes manifestation possible as the manifestation that extricates itself from Nothingness. Thus, each of the two orders the other and lets itself be ordered by the other. But the Nothingness of before is not a *state:* it is itself a possible, it is prolonged in the possibility of maintaining itself as such indefinitely. The veiled-being of the being to be unveiled is a to-come [*à-venir*] as much as a present: it is the possibility of being left veiled by me.

Thus, all that comes into the world through the pure upsurge of man comes as double possibility (Good and Evil, Truth-Error, the Beautiful and the non-Beautiful, and this including the details: to have children—to not have them; to speak—to keep silent; etc.), and for structural reasons. We speak on the ground of possible and rejected silence and if the possible silence was not the ground, the word in its nature would not be possible. In other words, the possible, being possible, may not be realized. But the nonrealization of the possible is not nothing, it is itself an opposite possible, an anti-possible; the possibility of the contrary. Therefore, if man is that existent who must receive nothing and by whom everything must *be done,* his act is perpetually a choice between the two possibles of a dyad (which does not mean deliberation or even thematization) and therefore, whatever he does, in the act itself, in the core of its essence, the opposite possibility is implied: freedom is not the choice between two or several *external* possibles with one being in external indifference [*dans l'extériorité d'indifférence*] towards the other. Freedom exists because any act, even completed, defines itself by the possibility of its opposite and because any *production* rises up on an anterior ground [*fond d'antériorité*] that defines it and is defined by it. Ignorance conditions knowledge and is defined by it, that is, both as possibility of knowledge and as possibility of remaining in ignorance. What then is the will to remain ignorant?

We must return to the veri-fying project. This project necessarily presupposes a taste for being. Indeed, through the unveiling, I make being *be*, I draw Being from its night; at this revealing moment, nothing is closer to me than Being because it is at the very point of becoming me or of my becoming it and because a simple nothingness, a nothing, separates us forever. I am *nothing* but consciousness of Being, *Nothing* separates me from Being. And since Being specifies itself as I specify my ends, this parallel makes me the accomplice of Being; I am *compromised* by Being. Besides, Being lends its being to my anticipations, which formally are subjective, insofar as they are objective. My subjectivity, while anticipating, borrows its being from Being, and, conversely, holds up to being a future being. Through Being my future is played out in Being; Being-in-itself has a future through me and is to come [*à venir*] to itself. As I invent Being starting from Being, and return to Being in order to sketch out Being on the surface of Being, I am exactly in the situation of the creator. But, conversely, by gathering itself together under my operational vision, by rising up congealed and indestructible under the temporal link that I bring about (*intuition is not instantaneous: all intuition temporalizes itself*), Being becomes the truth of my anticipation, or, rather, Being pours my anticipation into Being. Being inscribes in the In-itself the project of my for-itself. Therefore Being presents my project to me within the dimension of Being.

Enjoyment[20] is precisely this irritating and voluptuous proximity without distance of the For-itself to what is not itself. To enjoy a thing is to create it when it is. It is to illuminate it and to have what we are return to us in the dimension of the In-itself. It is to be as present to it as we are present to ourselves and yet be distinct from it.* Enjoyment is a unity, but one which is refused and which haunts duality like a ghost. Enjoyment is being nothing other than what we enjoy,

---

*In unveiling I create what is; when giving the truth, I give to you what is already offered to you. But, besides, I give it to your pure freedom since in turn you have to recreate what is (since freedom implies that the truth is never *given*).

and yet not being what we enjoy. It is the magical sketch of the identifying appropriation, in absolute proximity. To love the true is to enjoy Being. It is to love the In-itself *for the In-itself*. But at the same time it is to want that separation, that is, to refuse the identification of the In-itself with the For-itself because it would lose its compact density. It is to want to be the light sliding across the surface of the absolute density of being. To affirm is, therefore, through invented and verifiable anticipation and through the verifying return to Being, *to assume* the world *as if* we had created it, to take our place in it, to take the side of Being (to side with things), to make ourselves responsible for the world as if it were our creation. And, indeed, we draw it from the night of Being to give it a new dimension of being. To want the truth ("I want you to tell me the truth") is to prefer Being to anything else, even in a catastrophic form, simply because it *is*. But at the same time this is letting-it-be-as-it-is, as Heidegger says.[21] Therefore it means that we reject all identifying ruses (inauthentic knowledge: appropriation—to know is to possess, etc.). Authentic knowledge is abnegation just as is authentic creation (rejecting the subsequent link with what we have created). Abnegation: *to deny* Being, whether it is me, of me, or in me. From this, we can detect the origin of ignorance, prolonged by choice, and of lying.

In reality stubborn ignorance would have no basis if it did not contain the idea that nonrevealed being is a lesser being. And it is by denying ignorance that we combat it. "Of what use is it to you," we tell him, "not to look the situation straight in the face?" And as always, the "reasonable" point of view is both true and false. True in the practical, human world, in the world of means in which ontology is masked. False in the ontological world. It is indeed true that it is useless practically and in the human world to ignore a troublesome fact. But this is so because:

1. This is in a world where you have already chosen your ends, which supposes a certain organizing illumination of Being at the heart of which Being develops its coefficients of adversity in spite of you and forces you into catastrophic veri-

fication.* In other words, *practically* it is absurd: in La Fontaine's "The Enchanted Cup"²² some men decide not to drink from the cup because they do not want to know if their wives are cheating on them. But *if* their wives are cheating on them, they will sooner or later be affected: people will laugh at them, they will discover the adultery despite themselves, their wives will leave them, etc. When they got married they chose an undertaking involving two persons which stretches across their entire life and, whatever they may do, which is undergoing verification. They wanted happiness for two, their wives' fidelity, etc. And as they continue to want it, verification pursues itself inexorably. The only result of voluntarily stopping the verification while it is systematically possible (the cup is a symbol of a totality of organized operations) is that the verification is allowed to take place by itself as a logical consequence of each action, but a consequence which falls outside our project.

Thus chance comes to dominate verification—just as with Error. I refuse to *question* my wife about her conduct. Therefore I will not pursue the investigation. But the act of one day coming home earlier (Shahryar in *Thousand and One Nights*) can bring me face-to-face with adultery. At this moment, the discovery falls outside my action's definition, it results from a coming together of phenomena. In fact, everything follows logically: it is *because* I leave on a trip that my wife sees her lover at her home. And the whole is so rigorously logical that it is enough for a jealous husband to make a fictional trip in order for the series of facts to be *organized* as a unit in the form of a revelatory trap: he leaves *in order that* the wife can receive her lover, she sees him *because* the husband leaves, he left *in order* to return home unexpectedly; he comes home *in order* to surprise them, he surprises them *because* he left. But it suffices to have really left and come home by chance

---

*[What is lacking: distinguish between ontic truth and the truth of essences. When it is *gift*, truth is always a passage from the ontic to the essence. Blanchot: to name an object is to kill it as object and to transform it into an essence; to absorb its being in the word, to substitute the word for the thing.]

(for example, because we have forgotten something) for the discovery to become chance. Therefore, to want to not know [*ignorer*] is, ultimately, to want to place ourselves in the hands of chance.* (Moreover, we should also note the ambivalence of refusing to drink from the cup. We can see it also as a refusal to passively and contemplatively receive a knowledge that has not been created. Truth is act, my free act. The husband who refuses to drink refuses chance and passivity: he considers that the undertaking contains its own verification in itself and he rejects any truth that comes from outside, that does not surge up from the very heart of verification. In this state of mind we refuse to acknowledge anonymous letters, seeing them as interventions external to the very enterprise of living with a woman. The ambiguity of refusing to know appears, for example, when an acquaintance, who knows where my wife meets her lover, proposes to help me surprise her. Isn't this accepting a truth *external* to the undertaking, a truth that suddenly becomes like the appearance of God's point of view? Isn't refusal a voluntary closing of our eyes when the truth is manifest? Thus the husband's typical hesitation.)

2. To ignore is inefficient when dealing with already constituted truths, that is, those which develop their plenitude of being for others. What is the use of ignoring what others know? As we say in such a case, "The harm is done." My ignorance cannot take away a certain dimension of being from the In-itself since this dimension is already conferred on it by others. My ignorance can only affect *me* in my subjectivity. To ignore what is already revealed is not to affect Being with a lesser being; it is to affect myself with a lesser relationship with the world. It is to place me out of bounds. These are the reasons that justify the point of view of the *reasonable* man.

But, in fact, ignorance places itself on a radical, ontological plane. The point is not to unveil what is not yet unveiled by

*[The truth is not *true* if it is not lived and made. A revelation of infidelity is *false*. But contributing to the making and unmaking of a marriage on a daily basis (which is the responsibility of both) prepares you, the husband, for the precise moment of discovering adultery just when your wife is ready to commit it.]

anybody; the point is, regarding a particular region of being, to decide in general and a priori whether Being must or must not be revealed. And the refusal to know implies the original understanding that the unveiling of Being confers a supplementary dimension of being on the In-itself. The will to ignorance is first of all comprehension that Being exists less in its night. Being not *seen* collapses in Nothingness; it-is-in-order-to-collapse. Ignorance is the decision to let Being collapse. Willed ignorance is not even refusal to understand and to see (in the sense that people refuse to see what is unpleasant to them). The refusal to understand and see what is manifest at this moment stands in the same relationship to it as does the murder of my enemy to letting him, for example, drown without attempting to save him. The point is not exactly to destroy Being but to allow it to collapse in its night without intervening, by leaving to it all responsibility for this annihilation. (It's not I who kills my enemy. He shouldn't have got into that boat; it is his own fault that he died and I wash my hands of it.) Ignorance "washes its hands of it," it disputes human-reality's veri-fying mission. Being-in-itself cannot prescribe a mission to the For-itself. We will see that ignorance is contradiction and bad faith precisely because the For-itself prescribes this mission to itself by its very upsurge. Originally it is nothing if not unveiling transcendence of the In-itself, and the consciousness it acquires of itself is consciousness of self as it transcends and unveils Being.

Therefore, ignorance itself as a project is a mode of knowledge since, if I want to ignore Being, it is because I affirm that it is knowable. T. may well be sick and afraid of having tuberculosis but she refuses to see the doctor. Because obviously he can rid her of her fears but also *veri-fy* them. In this case the possible tuberculosis becomes definite, surges up in the universe with all its density, reveals itself through X rays and analyses, and becomes the meaning of symptoms isolated until now (fevers, etc.). It is. But if T. does not consult the doctor, we are dealing with a complex fact of minimization of being, which must be described: if ignorance *could be total* (if it could even ignore a possible tuberculosis), *real* tuberculosis could ultimately remain circumscribed in this being that we can just as well consider as nothingness of being. It *would be*, without being for anyone or for itself. Since it has not been taken into consideration, there is no obligation to *deal* with it. It would not force T. to choose herself against it, to assume it, to take her responsibilities for being ill with tuberculosis. To veri-fy is to create what is. T. refuses to take responsibility for allowing into the human world what has only the embryonic existence of a subterranean and nocturnal world. She refuses to choose herself as tubercular and to freely create tuberculosis. Therefore, in the formula "to create what is" she insists on the "to create" and drops the "is." She takes fright before her responsibilities (with respect to herself—in other cases it may be with respect to others) and her creative freedom.

Therefore—and we will develop this direction later—the fear of truth is fear of freedom. Knowledge commits me as accomplice of the surging up of Being in the world and places me before new responsibilities. The prudish wife refuses to *hear* the off-color remarks made in her presence; as far as she is concerned she refuses to make them *be*. For to listen to these remarks is a lesser way of *saying* them. (Bergson has clearly shown that we *repeat* the other's discourse within ourselves.)[23] This distinguished carnivore is eating a "chateaubriand," a strange object which bears the name of a writer and is sculpted out of an undefinable matter, but he refuses to visit the slaughterhouses (an *unhealthy* curiosity). If he goes there, the slaughterhouse surges up in the bourgeois world in full light: it exists, the chateaubriand is dead animal meat. But it is *preferable* to let the slaughterhouses remain outside of society, hidden in that obscure region where the very For-itself is parent of the in-itself; the killers of livestock are "brutes," obscure consciousnesses who do not master phenomena; the slaughterhouse is at the edge of the night, let it remain there. The gentleman-carnivore would be an *accomplice* if, through his knowledge, the chateaubriand transformed itself into dead flesh before the eyes of his guests.

34

Let us go back to T. She does not pretend that the tuberculosis will be suppressed by her ignorance, but only that it will not be integrated into the world where any being winds up, the human world. Even if tuberculosis remains at the embryonic stage, its effects will continue. But each one will be lived passively and without anticipation. This cough, this spitting of blood, this fever will be lived for themselves, and since only the anticipatory act allows us to *see* them, they will not be *seen;* they will go away opaque, isolated, barely noticed. They are like M.'s bad odor that N. did not notice because she did not want to perform a freely creative act of bad odor (to create the dirty, the ugly), and which consequently diluted itself into a vague annoyance without name and without memory. Ultimately tuberculosis will kill, but death is the perfect completion of ignorance, since death is the phenomenon that concerns me and that in principle I do not witness: for me there is no *truth* of my death. In this sense ignorance entertains a certain relationship with death which has to be brought to light and which will illuminate the notion of truth.

Dying is indeed that event of my subjectivity that I cannot know, and consequently has no truth for me. Yet since some of its aspects are knowable to others, this knowable which is not knowable for me deceptively defines an ignorance that is permitted to me. My death is the knowable fact that I have the right not to know. (The sophism: *I have the right* not to know it, because it is not knowable by me; and since it is knowable by others, it is "to be known" by them.) But immediately my death as a knowable not-knowable suspends all my veri-fying activities and leaves undecided the verifications in progress and the anticipations that are not confirmed and not invalidated. Death entails the indetermination of my knowledge [*connaissance*]; it plunges the totality of my knowledge [*savoir*] into ignorance. It also determines my ignorance vis-à-vis scientific research in progress. The existence of my death transforms knowledge [*savoir*] into non-knowledge [*non-savoir*]. From the point of view of death ignorance is legitimized.* Truth itself is affected: if I *can hold on* until death without veri-fying my wife's fidelity, I am saved, because suppressing the existing-unveiling of this infidelity removes all human meaning from the problem. I am going to die, my wife will die: the fact of infidelity will without a doubt retain its *being* but this being, since it will no longer exist for any for-itself, cannot be recovered and falls outside the human dimension of Being. But if, on the contrary, I must pursue my existence indefinitely, there is an infinite probability that I cannot ignore my wife's infidelity forever. Then the opposite happens: ignorance as a means of protection is contested by immortality.

---

*[The truth as constant revelation and as addition: we are *in the truth* but we do not look at it. At that moment it is *certainty*. But it becomes *truth in itself* if I give it to the other.]

Three types of future coming to Being-in-itself through the For-itself:

1. The present of Being-in-itself appears as future revelation. Being will discover what it *is*. The idea is the project of discovering this being; it is therefore intention towards this being. In the element of truth the present of Being is future to itself. Such is the static world that surrounds us (the closed book, the saucer that has been put down, the capped ink bottle, etc.).

2. The project is to discover a constant property of Being, but a property that appears only in certain particular circumstances (sodium always burns with a yellow flame, the combination of chlorine and hydrogen is always explosive when exposed to the atmosphere). A *characteristic* is intermediary between a present and a future. It is the unveiling of a *present* structure of Being but one which manifests itself at the moment of a specific contact with the world. It is a pure "present" to come [*à venir*] to Being but grounded strictly by its present. The creation of the *possible* of Being.

These two projects of Being starting from Being are the two possible forms of *Truth*.

3. The project is to *give* to Being a manner of Being which it does not yet have. The objective reality of the project is always supported by Being, for example, the being of the projected tool is the *true* being of iron or wood. (Invention and imagination are absolutely not the same. The imagination *invents nothing* because it diverts itself towards Nothingness. Invention transcends Being towards Being, it does not leave *reality*.)

Thus in each of the three cases Being supports the aim of being, which is the structure of the verifying or creative project. We notice the relationship between truth and creation. Consequently, it is clear that truth implies crea-

Therefore, to ignore is to ignore until death. Or then again to ignore (within a limited period of time) is to ignore until oblivion. (A whole structure to be analyzed. With the memory of covering up, forgetting through censorship. In each case, to forget is to *shroud*. Relationship of forgetting to shrouding. We *bury* a question, that is: we shroud it with earth, in the underground and nocturnal world of lesser being. Forgetting = symbolic death.) Finally a third structure: to ignore is to play on *finitude:* I cannot know *everything* at once. Therefore I devote myself to knowing in order to ignore because it is in my condition to ignore (physics, for example) in order to know (History, for example). To ignore, therefore, is to assume the point of view of finitude, oblivion, death, and passivity in the face of Being. T. will play with her *finitude* by engrossing herself in *verifying* her dramatic talent, because then there is no time to veri-fy her tuberculosis. Ultimately, it becomes hysterical distraction: to steadily and constantly illuminate one area in order to leave the rest in the dark. Ultimately, ignorance is negation; I ignore the burning and stinging sensations because I affirm that I no longer have a leg. T. will play with *forgetfulness* by letting the symptoms of her sickness plunge into Nothingness, by not totalizing them in the unity of an organic development. This spitting of blood

---

tion (that is, appearance of an unforeseen and free future through which Being comes to coincide with itself) and that creation implies truth (that is, that Being as it *is* holds up to Being the unforeseen future that is going to come to it and to inform it: sculpture is knowledge of marble, tannery knowledge of leather).

To be developed later on, irreducible ignorances:
a) the Other's point of view—the mystery of the big city;[24]
b) the point of view of the future;
c) the ground on which the chosen *form* carves itself out;
d) the insoluble problems—borderline situations, etc.

To distinguish ignorance as a necessary structure of truth and the action of mystery as alienation.

Ultimately, to know *everything* would be to do nothing (legends and myths). Why? Because total knowledge is *given* knowledge and therefore no more construction is possible.

is *forgotten*. Ultimately, forgetfulness is murder: that hypochondriac who hated her husband had *lost* her head [oublié *sa tête*]. T. will play with *passivity* by refusing all anticipation, that is, by denying her freedom in relation to the facts to be ignored. She *disregards* her cough; it is not present to her; she does not anticipate it as a cough: it does not come to illuminate her from the depth of the future; she lets it shake her as a series of *undefined* little spasms. Obviously passivity facilitates forgetfulness: we remember only what we have organized. Passivity, distraction, and forgetfulness are organically related. Distraction (engrossing ourselves in A) does not prevent B from coming to consciousness; consciousness is simply passive on that subject. (The frigid woman *experiences* pleasure but, engrossed in adding up her bills, does not involve herself in it and does not transcend the present content in order to expect even more in the future. Consequently, even if her body sighs and moves, she can forget this pure passivity.)

T. will play with her death because death, being both her unknowable and the irrefutable proof of her sickness, will suppress all possibility of proof and will be proof to *no one*. But the ignorant person takes as a project the point of view of finitude, in order to escape finitude; because truth reveals to her the finitude of the point of view. She takes the point of view of death out of fear of death; because if it is true that death suppresses truth, it is true that we die, and therefore, the placing of all truth out of bounds is reintegrated into the heart of truth. She takes the point of view of passivity because she is afraid of her body's passivity (a necessary structure of activity) which exposes her to microbes and, specifically, to tuberculosis.

Thus in ignorance we again discover a world torn apart by bad faith. In a word, ignorance is a refusal to be concerned with Being. It denies the relationship of internal negation that unites it to Being and makes it exist only as compromised by Being. It establishes between itself and the In-itself a pure relationship of indifferent exteriority. Therefore, truth and knowledge [*savoir*] are *discretionary* [facultatif]. But to affirm that external relationship, it must deny its ek-sistential structure[25] (it denies that it is the condition of veri-fication). And so, to avoid a compromising relationship with an in-itself, it transforms itself into in-itself. Of course, this modification is not truly achievable, but it treats itself as if it were an in-itself, and alienates itself from this in-itself that it presents. We are not dealing here with the futile chase after the In-itself-for-itself. The In-itself in question is pure in-itself as impermeable and indifferent [*imperméabilité d'indifférence*] to the other beings. As a result, in relationship to the For-itself the In-itself becomes as if it were itself a for-itself, as I have shown elsewhere.[26]

If I run towards the ditch hidden by branches to avoid the beater who is running after me,[27] I am indeed in a state of in-different exteriority in relationship to this ditch: it does not exist at all for me and my projects do not take it into account (the ideal of the project of ignorance is the ultimate ignorance [*ignorance-limite*] that does not even suspect that it ignores). But, at the same time, the ditch is awaiting me, is lying in wait for me. Since each step brings me closer to it and since for-me [*pour-moi*] these steps can neither bring me closer nor move me away from it, since I am ignorant of it, it represents in its exteriority the internal link of proximity. It awaits me, comes nearer and maneuvers my legs. This relationship of interiority in exteriority without reciprocity or, rather, this reversed and congealed image of the Project, is called Destiny. Ignorance is appeal to destiny. As is proven, by the way, by the comments that normally accompany the refusal to take care of ourselves: "We must let Nature take its course," or: "If it kills me, it kills me; if I survive, I survive." The ignorant person lives her death and, by refusing her freedom, she projects it on the world which reflects it back to her in the shape of destiny (Fatality). The world of ignorance is that of Fatality.

But, on the other hand, it is not true that T. can realize her ideal: that is, the ultimate ignorance which, in suppressing all relationship with Being, suppresses its own consciousness of ignoring and in this way symbolizes the rupture of any trou-bling relationship with the In-itself (especially the threats of the In-itself against the body). In fact, T. knows that she ignores. She even knows what she ignores. If she does not want to see the doctor, it is because she fears that he will *unveil* her tuberculosis to her. Therefore it is very specifically tuberculosis that she wants to ignore. Even more precisely, she *does not know* that she has tuberculosis: in this case, it would simply be appropriate (in her project of distraction) that she *forgets it.* She knows (or believes she knows) that tuberculosis is *possible.* She does not want to know if this tuberculosis is real. In a word, she wants to *forget* the possibility of this tuberculosis and to ignore the *truth* of this tuberculosis in case this truth were realized; she does not want to *confer* truth on this real tuberculosis. This can be expressed otherwise and we will see that this modification has its importance: she does not want the real being of tuberculosis to fulfil her empty intentions.[28] Indeed, T. cannot help but be entirely preoccupied by her tuberculosis. It is her *"idée fixe,"* her "obsession." But she is busy ignoring it, forgetting it. Therefore the organizing theme of her innermost events is Tuberculosis, transcendent being in itself.

As far as the thematic unity of her states of consciousness is concerned, tuberculosis has to have *a being.* But this being is a borrowed being. We now know what this borrowed being is. It is borrowed from the cough, the spitting of blood, etc. But unlike the real idea of tuberculosis, it does not return to these phenomena to illuminate them and to make a visible *form* surge up that includes them all. It remains a possible being (as *objective reality*), that is, a game of being and non-being; and as borrowed being it is sustained in being by the subjectivity that borrows it (it is possible because I project it). It is an in-itself that can be recovered by the for-itself: I can always transform it into subjectivity, i.e. I can perform the $\Sigma\pi\chi\acute{\eta}$[29] on it and see it suddenly as a pure noematic correlative of my consciousness. This results in another flitting game between in-itself and for-itself. Therefore I can *sometimes* consider it as being and then as not being, this is one possibility. And sometimes as in-itself (*possible* tuberculosis) and *then again* as NOT BEING IN ITSELF (the product of my anxiety).

40

Therefore, by means of this game, I undoubtedly maintain tuberculosis as *theme* of my *Erlebnisse*.[30] But at the same time this theme constantly has a lesser being than Being. It is my anxiety's noema, a sign's signification, the correlative of an imagining act; at the same time it is maintained in an indeterminate future because it is not the correlative of a single real operational act. As *present* (perhaps I do have tuberculosis), it is a *lesser being*; as *to come* [à venir] (I am going *to see* if I have tuberculosis), it is indeterminate; but an indeterminate future is a future that is not *my* future. In relationship to me it falls into exteriority; or, conversely, in relationship to my future I place myself in a state of indifferent exteriority, meaning that I purely and simply deny my transcendence.

In truth, it is just as impossible for human-reality to dispossess itself of its transcendence as it is to dispossess itself of its freedom. But it can project a transcendence *against its transcendence*. The totality of possible operations (going to the doctor, taking care of ourselves, etc.) will be blocked by other operations which are constantly projected. But since it suits the sick person to not realize that she *does not want* to go to the doctor (because that would suppose a clear-cut decision vis-à-vis her sickness and her assuming her responsibilities) these operations that interfere must appear to her as independent of her will: she is preventing herself from going there. For example (for the sake of the argument) she creates a value system which makes it more important to visit that friend than to go and see the doctor, or instead she is too busy socially; she is not *able* to go to the doctor, she *does not have the time.* Her body serves her (it mimics the sequence of events) and impossibility is the final unifying theme. Ultimately, transcendence hides *under impotence.* Thus, in order to confer a lesser being on what threatens me, I confer a lesser freedom on myself. And, finally, I hide the very idea of truth, which becomes the unveiling of a lesser-being by a lesser-subjectivity. A lesser-subjectivity because it is *less free* and incapable of ever performing genuine unveiling; a lesser-being because it is never given to intuition and it never transcends the *probable.*

41

Ultimately, truths are replaced by *opinion*.* Opinion is no longer free and verifiable anticipation of Being. It has lost its character *to come* [à venir]. It appears therefore as pure present or as pure contingency. We *have* an opinion, we do not know why. If we want to *explain*, we will seek the explanation contrary to the future one: the explanation by means of (past) causality. Opinion comes from heredity, our environment, education. At the same time—Plato is right—the correlative of opinion is the region of the play of being between Being and Non-Being[31] since *vision* is unveiling of Being and in this instance vision is rejected in the name of the inability to function. Therefore opinion is contingent belief about a ghost of being. I am not *responsible* for my opinions. Indeed, an opinion, being negation of the future and of all transcendence, is negation of freedom. Opinion being what it is, I feel no obligation at all to verify it. *Since* I am not responsible for it, why should I be obligated to find out if it is true? Ultimately, opinion is a pure *character trait*.

In conclusion, to want a world of opinions, is to want a lesser *truth*, that is both a lesser Being, a lesser freedom and a looser relationship between unveiling freedom and the In-itself. If I say that this is my opinion, I mean that I cannot stop myself from thinking in this way but I admit that you cannot stop yourself from thinking the opposite. Yet I do not judge it possible that someone can possess the *truth* on this question. Otherwise my *opinion* would be in error. Therefore I figure quite simply that the truth is not possible. For this reason the sick person who does not want to know that she has tuberculosis will say about doctors: Oh, what do they know! They all have a pet theory, etc. Therefore, the will to ignore the truth turns necessarily into the denial of truth.

These descriptions allow us to understand why we want to ignore. As we have seen, ignorance supposes a combination of three fears: fear of the unveiled In-itself; fear of the unveiling

*[Truth is norm as my demand [*exigence*] vis-à-vis the Other. I *give* it to him. I demand his *recognition* of my freedom as giver, that is, this is the *truth*.]

For-itself; fear of the relationship of the unveiling For-itself to the unveiled In-itself.

I. To not know is to want not to have to deal with pure Being but only with borrowed Being. What then does Being in itself have that can be so frightening? We want to stress here that the *original truth*, the most manifest truth, evidence that is as apodictic as the existence of the For-itself for itself, is the existence of the For-itself in the midst of Being or, rather, Being is irreducible to any subjective representation or content of this representation. The unveiling of this Being is therefore what is most immediate to the For-itself, which is conscious of itself in the face of Being from the moment of its surging up. But this immediate knowledge is on the contrary the most *veiled*. The manner of being of Being appears often as more manifest than Being itself. The red color of this flower appears inseparable from its form, except by means of abstraction. But we freely admit that it can be separated from its being (subjective sensation of redness) while its being-red is specifically the being of its manner of being.

Why then do we want to ignore *Being*? To understand this, we have to know *what* we want to ignore in Being. We have to go back to the description of Being as it appears to a veri-fying for-itself. At first it appears as non-deducible, as absurd, opaque, superfluous [*de trop*], contingent. Veri-fying human-reality, as it discovers Being, discovers its abandonment in the midst of the inhuman. For the world is both human and in-human. It is human in the sense that what is, surges up in a world that is born through the upsurge of man. But this never meant that it was *adapted* to man. It is freedom that is the perpetual project of adapting itself to the world. The world is human, but not anthropomorphic. In other words, it is on Being that the For-itself first grasps the silent refusal of its own existence. Since it is the being that *has* nothing without doing (condemnation to freedom), the world first appears to him as that in which nothing is given to man, within which man has no place unless he carves it out for himself. If Being

43

is superfluous in relationship to man, man is superfluous in relationship to Being. Being is the For-itself refused by the full density of Being. There is no room for the For-itself in Being. Being is a congealed hyperabundance that does not fill up.* [32]

Moreover, there is in the very In-itself a type of being that exercises an ambivalent mixture of attraction and repulsion vis-à-vis the revealing For-itself. Without a doubt the For-itself (attraction) would like to be In-itself-For-itself, that is, to assimilate the being of Being without losing its existence. But in pure Being that is not for-itself there is an element of repulsion. Being is terrifying. First of all, since it is not *for-itself*, it reveals itself in its being as pure and total obscurity. This means that it returns to the For-itself the dizzying image of a consciousness that would obscure itself totally, that is, a consciousness that would be for-itself consciousness of being unconscious, which would be consciousness of being irremediably *itself*. In a word, Being-in-itself is perfectly and totally manifest, there is no being-behind-the-scenes; there is no substance or another being behind it that explains it.

But in this very self-evidence is given obscurity to itself or absolute impenetrability, that is, mystery in the full light of day. Being delivers itself totally to the For-itself as itself, which means that illumination, instead of dissipating its obscurity,.illuminates it as obscurity. The Night of Being, the icy coldness of Being, is immediately accessible to us. Being appears to consciousness, which has set out to seek a recovery of the In-itself in For-itself, as an impossibility of being recovered, a refusal, a limit. Being is *indigestible.* At the same time, consciousness becomes conscious of the fact that it can neither produce nor suppress Being. Both creation and verification presuppose Being and are only a manner that Being has of coming to Being through the intermediary of a for-

*[Being in the world within a world that *refuses my existence.* This is the first *theme* of life in society; it is the very meaning of work.

1. If I do not act on the world, I die.

2. Accidents can kill me.

3. Antagonism of men and scarcity of goods. Ambivalence of social life. The other is he who shares my food with me and who steals it.] [33]

itself. Consciousness *discovers* Being as already existing [*étant-déjà*] and can modify in and through Being its manner of being. But Being in its being appears as the most intimate and necessary condition of the For-itself's existence and also as a nonmodifiable condition. In its upsurge, the For-itself, if it does not flee Being, discovers that without Being, it, For-itself, could not be because it exists only as consciousness (of) being conscious of Being. But there is no reciprocity since Being appears as *being-already* [étant-déjà].

Doubtless the For-itself confers a dimension of being on Being, namely, revealed-being, but this dimension is on the foundation of Being's already-having-been. Besides, and we will return to this, it is still not reassuring since the For-itself is conscious of freely confirming in its being a Being that is both opaque condition of the For-itself and negation of its very being. The For-itself helps its enemy to be. In addition Being is *irreparable*. Not that it cannot change by itself (motion), or be modified in its manner of being (alteration, construction, destruction). But suppose that consciousness, at a specific moment, has revealed being AB and suppose an AB that is changed or has annihilated itself. The revelation has undergone the modification of making-past [*passéification*].[34] And we know that passing into the past is transformation into an *in-itself that I have to be.* Thus nothing can change the fact that what has been hasn't been and, furthermore—since it is the past that *I have to be*—I have the responsibility, which I cannot refuse, to continue forever to make be what I have revealed. Since, furthermore, Truth ends up as a gift for the other, this revelation will be continued beyond my own existence, engaging my responsibility beyond my death.

Thus, in any *truth* there is an *irreparable* aspect. Each truth is both dated and historical, and it mortgages the infinity of the future; and it is *I* who confer this infinite existence of the "has been" on everything that I see (the In-itself by itself is what it is, is or is not, but could not have been). Therefore, in the face of the dazzling night of Being, consciousness, which is comedy, which is fake, which is makeshift, a coming to terms with self because it has to make itself be what it is, discovers a type of pitiless being without compromises or accommodations, the absolute and irremediable necessity of being what we are—forever and beyond all changes. Forgetting is a defense against the irreparable: it is the symbolic annihilation of the "has been" of Being. In a word, consciousness, which is not Being but which is overcome entirely by Being, struggles against that inadmissible necessity of assuming its responsibility of making be what it has not created.* I have shown that freedom *always* means assuming our responsibilities *afterwards* for what we have neither created nor wanted. (That car knocks me down; I couldn't avoid it. I'm missing an arm. My freedom begins there: assuming this disability that I did not create.) But it cannot escape from its condition.[35] At this point we had better describe the condition that Being sets down for the For-itself.

I have said that Being was the condition of existence of the For-itself and this is true. But there are two ways of being a condition. One is causal: A is condition of B because it engenders it or because, if I pose A, B follows necessarily. But the other is altogether different. When I say that the In-itself is indispensable to the For-itself, I do not mean by this that the In-itself *produces* consciousness (at least not the in-itself that is facing it) but just that consciousness only makes itself consciousness *through* the revelation of the In-itself. Now consciousness, being free, is the being through which the "in order to [*pour*] . . ." comes into the world (finality). Consciousness *is in order to. . . .*" But each one of its *projects* happens only on the foundation of the verifying revelation of Being, since it exists through this revelation. Therefore it reveals *in order to* exist. And, secondarily, since all action envelops a revelation, it reveals *in order to* pose its ends. The revelation is therefore consciousness' *means* of existing and also, secondarily, the *means of all the means*. Consciousness cannot choose an end without at the same time choosing the

*Freedom: assuming what we haven't created.

The inverted and inauthentic dream of freedom: to create without responsibility (the writer who does not want to be responsible—the schizophrenic dreamer).

truth, it cannot make itself be without making itself be before Being, that is, without revealing. But a *means* is itself an end. It is an end within the perspective of the ultimate end. Thus the revelation of Being is the fundamental end. Not the final end (we will return to this later) but the original end. Consciousness reveals *in order to* exist. There is no doubt that in order to exist, human-reality must also drink, eat, breathe. But in the drinking, etc., the revelation of Being is implied as an infrastructure. Therefore the fundamental end of consciousness is *imposed* on it.*

But whether it returns upon itself or searches around and about, it will never find *who* imposes this end on it. It *must* impose it on itself. It is in the situation of choosing an end freely that it cannot not choose. And yet this *not being able to not choose* does not belong to mathematical, causal, or dia-

---

*Three types of intuition and one type of correct operational indications:

1. Type of intuition: Being as given personally in behavior—perception—and to *life*.

2. Type of intuition: essences as Being's ways of being. Grasped on individual Being. The being-red of red.

3. *Meanings:* empty anticipating intentions, operational schemes (operations to be carried out, indications of possible intuitions). It is the future returning towards the present. *They are not intuitions* to the extent that it is I who live and project them. On the contrary, they are a priori the mark of absent intuitions or (symbols, etc.) of an infinite series of intuitions that cannot be carried out.

4. But these same *meanings*, from the moment that they define the behavior of the *other* and are encrusted in Being by the other, become objects sustained by the In-itself and open to a special intuition: the intuition of a signification as indications *in themselves* [en soi] of operations to be carried out, or, rather, intuition of the future [*futur*] as *given* future [*à venir*] in the present. If I take a flint or a piece of pointed iron and I use it as a knife, the meaning of *knife* as a piece of iron or flint is not given to me as a being, but only as a possible use that I project beyond Being. On the other hand, if the knife is manufactured by the Other, its being-knife as demand *on me* is given in its being. It is in reality the *project* of the Other, objectified by me in the form of the object and becoming meaning given by Others within my project. And this meaning *objectified* and held up to being, not by me but by Being, is the object of an intuition. There is intuition of the operational meaning of the *tool*, the *machine*, intuition of an object's signification in a society, a city, a civilization, intuition of the symbolic meaning of a flag.

47

lectical necessity but to the contingency of its being. It *is* a choice of revealing in the form of having to be it. Therefore the will to ignorance is (futile) revolt against a condition which is neither imposed nor thematically willed, and which is still a choice and engenders responsibilities. Here consciousness rebels against itself like the saints against God: why must I discover what horrifies me, etc. But Truth slides into this very revolt as a fundamental project.

II. Yet the unveiling of Being takes place in the element of freedom, since it takes place in and through the project. Therefore all knowledge of being implies a consciousness of ourselves as free. But this consciousness of being free is not a knowledge, but only an existence. Also there is no *truth* of consciousness (of) self but an *ethics*, in this sense that it is choice and existence giving itself rules in and through its existence in order to exist. But, on the other hand, the unveiling of Being presents freedom to *knowledge* in an altogether different form because Being always appears in the light of an enterprise and always reveals itself as a means in the light of an end. Truth, means of all means, constitutes true Being as a means or, which amounts to the same thing, as resolute refusal to be a means. During this walk, which is verification of a hypothesis (we have *consulted* [vu] the map, we want to make out the countryside with the help of the geographical outline), this path reveals itself as to be taken or not to be taken at the same time and by the same undertaking that, through verification of the geographical outline, constitutes it as going towards the east or the south. In a word, to drive east is the same as to be *taken*.

All truth is therefore a claim on my freedom, a mortgage on my future. And, since the totality of the means, united and hierarchized by the unity of a meaning, is identical to the projected end, and since the end is also the concrete and autonomous determination of freedom by itself in the world, the revealed truth reveals my freedom to me, not as something that *is* but as something that is perpetually demanded. Even before living in the universe of *Mitsein* (prohibitions and commandments), we live in a world of objective demands. The world is illuminated by my ends but, conversely, it is the world that sustains my ends in being and returns them to me in the form of objective-being. There is objectivity when the subject, transcending Being in a prefiguration of Being to come, appears to itself as object. The For-itself's freedom is knowable to it as the totalization of the demands of the revealed in-itself. And so knowledge of what is, is knowledge of what I want.

But since I *must will* the means if I want the end, I know what I want in the form of the hierarchical implication of what I have to will. And since what I want (the end) is strictly identical to the totality of what I *must* will (the whole of the means), there is a perpetual ambiguity here between demand and free choice. If I *choose* to be at work at eight o'clock, my choice can also appear to me as that delightful being-to-come that is my presence at work and, moreover, as the totality of means: going to bed early, hearing the alarm, washing, getting dressed, lighting the fire, etc.—that is, as all the future mortgages on my present freedom. Truth presents my freedom to me in the form of a demand that the world establishes on me. Or, rather, I know Being-in-itself as perpetual demand. The easier the realization (repetition of a daily act, for example), the more the grouping of means will occur continuously and spontaneously; in this case I keep the end in sight as focus of the means and the *truth* of the means remains implicit. They do not posit themselves for themselves. (I want to light a cigarette: I have to look for the package, strike the match, etc., but the objects are in their place, the acts perfectly known and regulated. Therefore the end appears and my freedom appears to me in the form of free project and not as a demand. That is, the final object, the lit cigarette, the flavor, taste of the smoke, is indeed *to be realized* but not in the form of a hypothetical imperative. On the contrary, it does so in the form of recovery of the In-itself by the For-itself: I seek myself in the world in the form of an object of the world. Coincidence with myself comes to me in the form of tobacco flavor to be tasted.)

But the more the means reveals itself as distant from the

end, which is difficult to invent, the more truth reveals the coefficient of adversity of things, their refusal to be means. And the more the *end* appears in the form of dialectical unity of means and consequently the more it is demand, that is, hypothetical imperative. But the hypothetical imperative distinguishes itself only in its expression of the categorical imperative. Indeed it is in its universalizing thematization and as a pure possibility, not yet chosen, that it announces itself: "If you want x, you have to will y." In lived reality, x is always "already chosen" and is lived as the great present and future form, the environment in which I grasp the means. Thus the means appears at this moment as a categorical imperative. Since I *already* want *x*, the object is given in categorical form: in the general perspective of your choice, you *have to* will me. Therefore, in favorable cases, the unity of means is undifferentiated background in the process of becoming, on which *the end* is realized as *form*; in difficult cases, the end is background and pure illuminating environment from which the means detaches itself as particular form, that is, as a special demand of Being.

This is why *I must* is constantly used in current speech where we would expect *I want to.* A typical conversation: the patient is agitated, becomes nervous: "I *must* be up tomorrow to receive P." The friend answers: "Not at all; P. will understand perfectly, you don't need to, etc." In short, an attempt to disarm the categorical imperative by showing it to be an unnecessary means. My desire throws me into the world and the world returns it to me in the form of demands; I no longer recognize it. In this sense, the project of ignoring Being, of masking it, of giving it a lesser being, is the project of giving my desire a permanent character of desire, that is, *not* to leave it as an immanent subjectivity that has never existed but to maintain it as pure immediate contact with the desirable *to come* [à venir]. My desire recognizes itself in the desirable and finally projects, in *satisfaction*, the unveiling unity of the desiring For-itself and the desirable In-itself. Thirst is absorbed in the drink that takes its meaning from the thirst. Thirst does not choose to annihilate itself but to be pure incorporating revelation of the qualities of water, of wine, etc. But as soon as we reveal the world, the organization of means as a series of imperatives substitutes itself for the pure unveiling adaptation of desire and the desired. The project's original watchword, transforming the In-itself into the For-itself in and through its destruction and systematic assimilation in the light of desire—to give to the For-itself the cohesion of the In-itself by making the desired be drunk by the desiring one—is modified as soon as it begins to be realized and throws us into the world of imperatives and means.

In truth, we are dealing with an absolute structure of freedom, since the end is to come [*à venir*] and is therefore necessarily beyond the world and to be realized through it. But it is precisely this demand that I deny in positing the world of desire as an absolute [*dans la position absolue du monde du désir*]. The world of desire or the world of reflection: I want to see myself in things, dissolve myself in things, dissolve things in me. In fact, this world could only be realized in the immediate because, as soon as the end is realized through means, it is other.[36] Therefore there is constant mystification of desire. (Another mystification: satisfied desire changes itself, while it is satisfying itself, into extinguished desire, and at the very moment that the end is totally realized I am already beyond my desire.)[37] Everything happens as if man's function were to accumulate means and as if the end were the means making him accumulate these means.

The young person protests against this mystification. Antigone: *I want everything immediately.* This means: I exclude *Being* as radical alteration of my desires. To refuse Being (to ignore), is to want to be the freedom that *enjoys* to the detriment of *the* freedom that *does*. The underlying idea: the means dishonor the end. (Well, if I have to do *all of this* to satisfy my desire, I prefer to abandon it.) This ignorance can only be fully achieved in a world of oppression. Indeed, in this world only the oppressor can be in immediate communication with his end: the kingdom of means is left to the oppressed. As is the case in the child's world and that of the (oppressor's) young daughter. But because freedom is the impossibility that anything is ever *given* to man and because freedom is the necessity to work, the rejection of the world of means is the rejection of freedom. The will to ignore is therefore the refusal to be free.

Furthermore, it is, as we noted above, the refusal to face our responsibilities. Since indeed, Being appears, in principle, as that for which we have to assume responsibility without having wanted it, the For-itself can project the veiling of Being in order not to be obliged to assume it. As a bourgeois I want to ignore the proletariat's condition in order to ignore my responsibility for it. As a worker, I may want to ignore this condition because I am in solidarity with it and its unveiling obliges me to take sides. I am responsible for everything to myself and to everyone, and ignorance aims to limit my responsibility in the world. Thus the geography of my ignorings [*ignorances*] represents negatively and exactly the finitude of my choice of being. Ignoring [*ignorance*] = denial of responsibilities. And conversely: the fewer the responsibilities the less we need to know; that is, if society puts you in a situation where your responsibilities are taken away (the "kept woman"), you are not at all worried about the *Truth*; you get your truths from others just as you get your money from others. The woman's ignorance is not a pure and accidental lack of being informed, it comes to her from outside and it changes her internally, as the loss of all control over the world. In exchange (in the best of cases) she is given at least the illusion of an immediate contact between her desire and the desirable. At this level, then, what is the ideal world projected by the will to ignorance?

1. What we don't know doesn't exist.
2. What we know exists only insofar as we know it.
3. We choose at will to know or not to know.

Therefore ignorance is wishing for a world where unveiling = creation. It reverses the formula of Truth: create what is. It postulates that nothing *is* except for what we create. It postulates therefore:

52

1. that desire is the universal motor of creation and that it is creation of the desirable;

2. that the desirable is in the element of the In-itself. In other words, it falls outside of the For-itself into Being. It possesses the moment of autonomy.

3. But it is recovered by the satisfaction of desire and becomes a mental event. It returns to the For-itself. Valéry's text in the first issue of *Arts et métiers graphiques:* "READABILITY IS THAT QUALITY OF A TEXT that foresees and facilitates its consumption, its destruction by the mind, its transubstantiation into an event of the mind." For a general definition of ignorance it would suffice to replace *readability* by *digestibility* and *text* by *world.* As a result, the moment of responsibility is limited to the stage of Being's independence and it is quickly suppressed by the assimilation of Being to mind.

In other words, ignorance is nostalgia for Hegel's absolute-subject, which as pure, unique consciousness produces the world by means of unsheathing [*devagination*] and reincorporates it through sheathing again [*re-invagination*].[38] Ignorance is the refusal to have responsibilities except for ourselves. And this refusal is necessarily accompanied by the outline of a positive world of the absolute-subject: the world of *dreams.* It is not true that the schizophrenic prefers the dream because he appears there as a millionaire, an emperor, etc. He prefers the world of dreams because Being *is* in it only to the exact extent that it is revealed: he prefers the *poverty* of Being because Being is a *lesser being,* which is immediately reabsorbed in subjectivity and because between the desired being and the desiring being there is no intermediary.[39] There is no doubt that we deprive ourselves of the satisfaction (of the desire), but this is deliberate because satisfaction is suppression of the desire and mystification. The world of dreams is a world of desire that wants to remain desire and let itself be announced by a being which is the exact counterpart of desire.

Innocence is a form of ignorance which is very dear to human societies. We can see why:

1. Innocence = absence of responsibilities. An innocent

person is someone who is not responsible for this crime or that mistake. We maintain certain beings artificially in a state of nonresponsibility in relation to the world (women, young girls, children). For this reason these beings are the living image of what man would like to be. They demonstrate the possibility of having no connection with the world.

2. As a result innocence = ignorance. Ignorance of the "realities" of the world which are *"ugly."* Man is forced to know, but in the very heart of the world he installs the symbol of this ignorance for which he is nostalgic. And he knows that the ignorant one remains ignorant of him. *He* knows that he has genitals, etc., but he makes himself exist for another as ignored in his reality.* He creates the ignorant one as innocent so he can exist somewhere as ignored in his ugliness (something he cannot ignore). He entrusts someone in his place to be ignorant of what he knows. Which explains the scandal that results when we stain ignorance, the innocence of innocents: it is one way of making my sex and my vices exist a second time in the world.

3. And of course the world of innocence will be that of dreams (fairy tales for children, "What do young girls dream about").

We complete the construction by justifying innocence over knowledge. There exists a *true knowledge* in the ignorance of the innocent person. Through a dialectical reversal, not knowing [*ignorer*] is the best way of knowing. At stake here are moral and ontological concepts: because we posit an ethics of ignorance, we posit a world that should be one of inno-

---

*Feminine intuition as a type of ignorance that knows because it is ignorance.

But in reality ignorance is not a vision of the Good: it is a non-vision of evil. How can I see the Good as the effort of the man who is besieged by Evil (struggles against temptations, etc.—I am thinking here of Good at the level of the myth of innocence) if I do not see Evil? But innocence is a Manichean operation that does not restore the Good directly but rather by applying itself to not knowing [*ignorer*] Evil. Then Evil is no more than what *prevents* the Good from being completely. Evil is the negative and ignorance is negation of the negation. Through the restoration of a primitive state in which Evil was not and Being was the Good (Paradise before the Fall).

cence (absolute-subject, unique consciousness, recoverability of Being, irresponsibility). And since innocence is intuitive grasp of this world, we posit that this world truly *is*. The lesser value of the real world then becomes lesser being. Practical activity, struggles, fears, interests prevent us from *seeing* the world as it is. The irresponsible person *sees* it: for example, Dostoyevski's Idiot. Through a secret harmony he is especially adapted to a lost innocence which is only masked by each one of us (i.e., our secret desire to ignore). For example, being ignorant of [*ignorant*] Evil, he sees only the Good in the evil person, and this is pure wisdom precisely because Evil is only an appearance, a misfortune, an accident, and at bottom the worst criminal is still capable of goodness.

At the same time innocence itself does not know [*s'ignore elle-même*]: the young girl is ignorant of her sexuality [*ignore qu'elle a un sexe*], for example. And, out of respect for her ignorance, I also place myself in the position of ignoring it. But, consequently, both of us suppress it in order to arrive at the true relationship between people, which is asexual. Through this we realize that the true human relationship is to be angels.[40] Therefore the dialectical reversal consists of making of ignorance a means of knowing. To know is to be ignorant of [*ignorer*] (the discovery of life's ugliness obscures the pure vision of beauty) and to not know [*ignorer*] is to know. Thus man selects certain oblates, virgins in spite of themselves, and imposes on them the function of symbolizing, in the midst of this scientific and technical world, absolute ignorance as superior to all forms of knowledge. This will allow him to relate each specific decision to ignore this or that to an original innocence, which is both incarnated value and intuition of Being. When a bourgeois decides to ignore the conditions of the working class or the origin of steak, he thus becomes like a young virgin. Historically, moreover, in Genesis knowledge is presented as a fall: the tree of knowledge was a trap.

III. The result is a new manner of justifying ignorance: yes, the world must be *known*, Truth is the fundamental structure of the world; without truth the world cannot be. But just because the Truth must be, it does not follow that it must be for me. Adam and Eve can dispense with knowledge because God knows for them. As a result, because divine consciousness is creative and verifying, being and truth become one. Therefore truth is pre-human. Rather than truth coming to being through man, we see that the true-being of Being is already fully constituted *before us*. From then on we can only be passive towards Truth: contemplation. The link of truth with freedom is broken. Therefore we have to *receive* Truth. But, as a result, Truth is separated from verification. True is what is communicated to us by the existent qualified to make the True exist. All we have to do is to recognize this existent. And the mark of this existent is Value. It is its Power, its Force, its Goodness, etc. that guarantee its power of truth. This would be God. But it could just as well be Hitler or Stalin. Consequently we are no longer responsible for the True. They give us the True according to our needs. All we have to do is to ignore what has not been given to us. In this case our nature turns out to be ignorance (because to make truth come about is to create and this we don't do), and each truth is a divine grace that was not our due.

Human-reality is indeed perfectly aware that to make the truth exist means giving a new dimension of being to Being. He who discovers an unpleasant truth holds himself responsible and is held responsible for the unpleasantness of the truth. Woe to him who provokes a scandal. According to a common myth exploited by dozens of novelists a certain penetration of Being is punished: one goes mad or becomes a criminal (the myth of the mad scientist, the man struck by lightning, by madness, for seeing into the heart of things, the myth of the science that brings unhappiness). A contemporary reflection on atomic science: "Today's scientists have discovered that Science could be transgression." As if the discovery of atomic energy made the scientist responsible for the potential death of humanity. Indeed, all contact is promiscuity: revealed being *rubs off* on revealing Being. If I have *seen* Being, I am magically impregnated by whatever affects

Being. Creating what is, I am what I create. There is something perfectly right in this statement: I discover Being through my project, and truth, before becoming *the* universal truth—through gift and verification across the entire human adventure—is *my* truth. It appears to me according to what I have chosen to be and according to my point of view. It could not appear to another. It is absolute truth to this absolute subject.

In this sense, "to each his own truth" is a correct turn of phrase because each person defines himself by the living truth that he unveils (that is, equally through his undertakings, because one implies the other). As we say, it is no accident that he who sees only the ugliness of the world sees nothing else. And if he sees only this, it cannot leave him unaffected. But in this sense only, because if verification exists, it remains true that what I could see alone, I can *make* everybody *see.* It remains true that I am him through whom the Truth comes into the world and to everyone. I may be a prophet of doom, I may be Cassandra. And I feel myself to be a Cassandra, because, if I did not exist, if I did not point it out, that being would not exist for others. I am the means that such a being has chosen to rise up in the human world.

As a result, this type of ignorance aims at two goals: (1) to relieve the one who speaks, of the responsibility for what he says (revelation); (2) to avoid the *vision* of Being, which is magically the most compromising form: I do not mind *knowing* but I do not want to *see.* For knowledge is a type of empty intention, it aims at a being to come or a past being, in any case a borrowed being. Vision, on the other hand, fills knowledge with Being. I do not mind knowing that Peter is dead, but I do not want to *see* him dead, that is, through my existence, to allow his death to exist as unveiled-being. I do not mind obtaining a ready-made truth and using it as means for my action but without opening it, without *realizing* it. Proust and the inconstancies of the heart: his knowledge of his grandmother's death is a closed truth, a truth for others, not compromising.[41] One day he *realizes* it, that is, the definite absence of his grandmother, her no-longer-being in the world, is absence unveiled in things. How many truths useful for our action and constantly employed by us are thus closed truths, sealed letters. We foolishly call this "not having imagination." We say that the judge who condemns a criminal to ten years in jail does not *imagine* the ten years of suffering. It is not that he does not *imagine* them, he refuses to verify them (visits to prisons, etc.). Thus an *"idealist"* type of truth is created, i.e., truths that are statements about Being without contact with Being. Thus is created a kind of thought making truth the product of reasoning and of discourse that refuse intuition's fundamental revealing value.

Thus there appears a type of man who *chooses to be abstract*, that is, to *know* the true in its strict form of instrumentality and without disclosure. Knowing without seeing: this is abstraction. It is possible only through the *Mitsein.* The abstract man profits from the revelations of others and he entrusts others with the veri-fying of his anticipations. The abstract man thinks upon the thought of others, that is, on revelations that he does not bring about. He is like the mathematician who places himself at the level of complex formulas containing the operations to be undertaken, but who never carries out these operations. The abstract person *reasons* not because he does not see but *in order not to see.* Similarly, he is himself abstracted: for example, he *eats abstractly,* in a state of abstraction in relation to the revealing value of eating.* He eats while reading, while talking, like the frigid woman who makes love while thinking of something else. The abstract man is the man who always thinks of something else in order to flee from the revealing value of his present behavior, whatever it may be. The abstract man is absent. For the abstract man Truth is neither Being nor the unveiling of Being, it is knowledge *about* Being, in the absence of Being. Thus total Truth becomes the totality of all knowledge and Being falls outside of truth, it is no more than the obscure foundation to which all this knowledge relates. Ultimately, for the abstract man, knowledge replaces Being. He is an

*Transition to the second type of truths: the truths about Others.
Transition to the second structure of truth: truth as gift.

idealist out of fear of Being-in-itself. For the enjoyment of Being he substitutes his simply aiming at it. Thus he can *know* everything while being ignorant of *everything.*

Therefore ignoring is fear of Being or fear of freedom or fear of the revealing contact with Being or fear of all three at once.

On Necessary Ignorance

However this project of maintaining ignorance can be developed only on two conditions. First, ignorance has to be at the starting point of Truth (we have already seen this); second, all truth must always be surrounded by ignorance. We will study this question now. It amounts to stating that ignorance must *inhabit* all truth not only as the soil from which Truth draws its origin and can be rediscovered in transcended form as its temporalization (*becoming* truth: all truth is ignorance having become truth; the necessary temporalization of truth or verification: freedom as foundation of truth requires that it itself emerge from ignorance) *but also* as its finitude, as its shadowy side. We know that, if all determination is negation, man is the being who interiorizes his finitude. Truth, as human undertaking, is interiorization of ignorance because ignorance is the finitude of truth. To know *this*, is *to know only* this. It is to choose to see *this* to the exclusion of all the rest (for the time being), it is to make *this* appear on the rest of the world envisaged as *ground*, that is, undifferentiated plenum of being (ignorance). It even means affirming that every *this* in the world of Being exists as appearing on an undifferentiated ground. But there are still many other aspects of ignorance as finitude of truth, and we will describe these next.

I. Freedom is the foundation of knowledge.[42] The limit of knowledge is also freedom. Freedom does not create finitude; on the contrary it is through finitude that there is freedom. As freedom I am only insofar as I am a contingent point of view that is not the foundation of its being and is in danger in the world. And there is truth only in relation to this point of view that makes a world exist and successively unveils itself. *But* finitude is interiorized by choice. In other words, *to choose* is to make *my* finitude exist concretely *for me*. Freedom is interiorization of finitude. Man is his own determination to himself, i.e., his own limitation, i.e., his own negation. Choice is choice of what I am to the exclusion of all the rest. In this sense the initial choice is already assumption of what was already before: it makes my contingency exist as necessity of contingency. It returns to what was still only being (and not in the form of "there is") to confer on it a meaning and a temporalizing vection [*vection temporalisatrice*].[43]

Therefore the choice to reveal *a* truth is always interiorization of *lack of knowledge* [*non-savoir*]. In *all* truth there is an internal relationship to my own freedom. Indeed, to the extent that *my* freedom interiorizes finitude but at the same time posits a future of freedom in relation to the finite present (and even outlines the infinite infinitude through the ek-static outline of temporalization), freedom posits an undefined *future in which it will be* a conscious and determining freedom *in relation to* the present conceived as free unveiling of the In-itself. Therefore, in the very present, at its core, there is a double structure. It is on the one hand an absolute insofar as it temporalizes itself starting from a future [*à-venir*] that is my most immediate and most concrete possibility; and at its core it also possesses a *destiny*, which is the necessity of becoming a *thing* for a freedom that is *my* freedom insofar as it is unpredictable, that is, my future freedom returning to the present that I am living and will have become past.

Each project as the living, ek-static synthesis of the three concrete ek-stases of temporality is interiorization of finitude and *at the same time* consciousness that the free-being of future freedom re-exteriorizes this finitude. The "to live A," in the absolute and unique unveiling project, is already a future "having lived A" that is grasped as a "having lived only A." And since all freedom is unveiling, it is *from the point of view* of another as yet undetermined veri-fication that my present truth will be *re-exteriorized* finitude. Which means objectively that all revealed truth is both absolute and indeterminate. What is the criterion of truth? There is no doubt on this point: it is *Being* as presence. I have already explained that we are as sure of the presence of Being as we are of our own existence. Thus, when the unveiling takes place, we grasp [*nous saisissons*] Being and we can no more doubt it than we can doubt the *I think* (the structures are related).

Therefore *I grasp* [je tiens] the truth; it is absolute, it is the unquestionable result of the process of verification. Evidence [*l'évidence*] as *unique* criterion of the truth is not at all grasping a certain stamp of truth on an idea. Evidence is Being itself insofar as it appears to the For-itself. But at the same time that this evidence delivers Being to me and through it I protect myself absolutely against any future, whatever it may be. (*Verum index sui*[44]—or rather it is not the truth that indicates itself as truth, nor the idea that indicates itself as true by some mark of its conformity with Being; it is Being that indicates its presence in truth in the evidence. In any case, for any future, for any Other, what is unveiled to me at this instant, in the process of verification, *was*—as a correlative of "whatever I may want and think of myself later, it is absolutely true that I want and will have wanted such and such a thing in my present project.") At the same time, therefore, as I protect myself against any future through the determined interiorization of my finitude and the claiming of my right to *see only this*, my pure future, as undetermined possibility of a future beyond this one, also constitutes an outside for my project (which in my memory will become an in-itself completed from the outside) and through this an undetermined outside for *my truth*.

Indeed, this future freedom is *this other* that I am to become for myself. It is a very specific other: what I will call "the other without the reciprocity of alterity." He is *for me* completely an other, but for him I am *the same*, undoubtedly not in the sense that he would penetrate the absolute of my present *Erlebnis* but in that it will be entirely familiar to him, in that he *will have to be it behind himself*, in that whatever he does he will have to assume it, that is, to re-interiorize a finitude that I prescribe for him from this moment. I am not

61

responsible for what this alter ego *will do* next year (except if I can already foresee this, prepare for it, and agree to it) but he is responsible for me, in relation to him I am like the under-age child in relation to its father: he is committed to me and I am not committed to him, he pays for me and I do not pay for him.

This will pose ethical problems concerning *commitment, the pledge,* etc. For the moment our only concern is with truth;[45] the other that I will be for myself is obliged to accept the truth that I now discover, to the extent that it is verified and always verifiable truth. If it were no longer verifiable, my future ego could even doubt it. *One day* I saw so-and-so pass by. Let us admit that this was *true* in the sense of *verum index sui*. It was self-evident [*J'ai eu l'évidence*]. But it is impossible to experience it again. If the memory is sufficiently distinct, if it can give itself in its fullness to the new ego's reflection, it will itself be *index sui*, that is, an intuition of the memory of an evident fact is itself an evident fact [*une évidence*]. But if the memory is more or less the object of empty intentions—because of resistances, systematic forgetting, etc.—the empty intention no longer carries conviction if verification is impossible. In other words: the lived unveiling, entering into memory, becomes unveiling *in itself*. As such, it can be unveiled in turn; it is presence to the remembering consciousness of the in-itself that I have been. And as in-itself it is *index sui*. But if it is only intended, it has the same degree [*statut*] of probability as the transcendent In-itself that I am not.

But if we suppose a verifiable truth which as such imposes itself on consciousness as *to be assumed*, we do not know *from what perspective* it is to be assumed. Indeed, the future freedom will grasp it from within its new project and integrate it into this project. This means that it will confer a new meaning on it. Indeed, I have shown that the present does not determine the being of the past but its meaning;[46] it is true once and for all that this adolescent that I have been has had a religious crisis at the age of fourteen. But the importance of this crisis in the concrete totality of my finitude is to be determined bit by bit. Similarly, *this* is an indubitable truth, but its meaning remains *open*. Specifically, it remains *undecided* whether it will have a relationship of exteriority or interiority with truths to be discovered later, that is, whether it will place itself alongside my other future knowledge or whether it enters into a synthetic totality of *knowledge* as an imma-nent secondary structure.

For example, Euclidean geometry, Cartesian analytic ge-ometry, Newtonian physics are *true*. But their relationships to subsequent truths differ. For example, the relationship of Euclidean geometry with non-Euclidean geometries is one of exteriority. These are varied possibilities of construction start-ing from diverse and mutually exclusive postulates. And we can undoubtedly speak of a totality that would be the totality of geometries obtained by the systematic exhaustion of all pos-sible postulates. But this totality is a pseudo-totality: it only means that *there are no* other postulates, hence other geome-tries; it does not mean that these geometries possess an inter-nal unity. On the contrary, Newtonian physics is integrated into modern physics which, without rejecting it, imposes an internal limitation on it: it becomes a physics of appearances, physics of the *as if*, a physics of specific cases. And it maintains a *being* precisely because there is a being of appearances. But its ability to isolate a truth that limits itself is broken, in the same manner that Hegelian negativity makes the barriers ex-plode: it is *aufgehoben*.[47]

Besides, a truth appears at the heart of unverified and per-haps unverifiable anticipatory presuppositions to which it communicates its (borrowed) being and which confer on it more and more ample margins of meaning [*signification*]. A truth that has appeared in a system of beliefs and myths can confirm these beliefs and myths (that is, we *decide* to stop the verification). For example: to Leibniz the discovery of infini-tesimal calculus appears as *proof* of the truth of his metaphysi-cal views. Conversely, this means that Leibnizians confer a realm of metaphysical meaning [*signification*] on this cal-culus. But, precisely because these meanings [*sens*] are not verified, the alter ego[48] will always be able to drop them and to integrate the truth in other philosophical-mystical systems. For example, Archimedes' law functions within different perspectives today than when it was discovered. Being discovered at a time when it is believed that bodies have natural habitats is not the same for the *meaning* of a truth as being preserved at the time of the Galilean and Cartesian mechanics. For example, the *pressure* that a submerged body withstands is understood and grasped differently: in Archimedes' time, it still is somewhat *alive;* in Descartes' time it is a manifestation of inertia. But at its deepest level the intuition remains, and, to go farther, already *for Archimedes* it even contains, implicitly, a negative denial of the meanings [*significations*] that it allows to be confirmed and that give it *its horizon of meaning.*

Thus each truth is simultaneously closed and open. It appears as the presence in person of the In-itself, with a circular horizon of meanings [*significations*] that close the look [*regard*]. And it is simultaneously open insofar as these meanings are not verified but only presumed, and insofar as it remains undetermined what subsequent use the alter ego, and later on *the others*, will therefore make of this truth. Objectively, this means that there is a necessary and dialectical antinomy of truth: there is only total truth (thesis)—there must be partial truths (antithesis). This is resolved as follows: in a semidialectical world having a fibrous structure and revealing itself to a detotalized totality and to subjectivities in process [*en cours*], any appearance is in a sense *total* because it delivers *all* of Being to a finitude that interiorizes itself in an absolute *Erlebnis.*

And, in another sense, it reveals itself *with the world as ground*, that is, on the ground of the unity of all Being united into a world. And this is its *opening* because its *order* and its *place* are not determined. And it would be incorrect to say that this order and place are part of its inner determinations (in the sense that we call truth that is not in its place an error) just as it would be incorrect to say that they do not matter to it at all. It depends. The future will decide. For example, for Euclidean geometry it is only an exterior event [*aventure*] to not be *all of geometry*. It is an interior event for Newtonian physics to not be *all of physics*. Thus, without taking away its kernel of obvious revelation, truth always reveals itself against a horizon of ignorance which constitutes its possibilities of development and life. Verifying human-reality recognizes this ignorance in generosity and liberation. Liberation because it gets free of the possibilities of secondary errors (dealing with marginal meanings [*significations*]); generosity because truth is thus given to the alter ego I will be and to the others by *allowing them to make of it what they will*.

This can be expressed otherwise, that is, not by reference to the future *alter ego* but to the present others. In fact a truth appears in three possible ways: it is *my* truth; it is truth that has become for the other; it is universal truth. It is *my* truth, meaning that the unveiling takes place through me, in my climate, in relation to a certain horizon of values, ends, and meanings [*significations*]. When I give it to the other, I can have the intuition he sees because, the other being as real as myself and as Being-in-itself (I discover myself as the for-itself which exists opposite the In-itself and among other for-itselves), I apprehend him immediately as an observing look. I point out the object to him and he looks at it. He looks at it on the tip of my finger. But from then on, the object develops a dimension of being which escapes me a priori.

I have pointed out such and such a *red* flower (a rare specimen, for example, whose flowers are normally yellow); therefore I have made the other discover that *there are* red flowers of this type. But, as a result, its red color escapes me in part because I do not know what the other is doing with it. I am banished from the living integration of the red into another system of truth. I do not know in what climate it reveals itself as red, of what meanings [*significations*] it becomes the focus, I do not know what the other *is doing with it*. Henceforth, my own truth becomes incommunicable to me, it lives outside of me under other skies, with other dimensions, and Being escapes me. And, consequently, my truth, as living intuition and interiorized finitude, receives an external limitation: it *is only* my truth *any more*. (The other goes beyond me. As in reviews: "He has properly understood that . . . but he has not understood that. . . .") And, undoubtedly, in dealings with the other he can *return to me* what he stole from me by in turn showing me what he has seen beyond me. But he can also not do it: therefore my truth is limited by the freedom of the other. And above all, he cannot do it completely because certain anticipating implications and even certain revealing visions are not thematized for him.

Therefore, all truth is presently provided with an outside that I will forever not know [*ignore*]. This time an insurmountable ignorance constitutes my truth. Thus, at the moment I can proudly affirm that I am the one through whom this truth surges up in the world, in modesty I must freely recognize that this truth possesses an infinity of facets that escape me. Some men keep their truths to themselves just to avoid bringing these multiple facets, these dimensions of flight, into existence. But, as a result, they lose the benefit of a gift, which is the passage of intersubjectivity to the absolute and, besides, it is enough that these facets be virtually implied by the Other's existence for any truth to acquire an outside by itself. Therefore the attitude of generosity throws the truth to others so that it becomes infinite insofar as it escapes me. Besides, this infinity often remains potential because the others, even if they have understood the truth that I give them, *do nothing with it* and only *repeat* it. But this stage is temporary. This is the source of the creator's pure pride: he gives a truth that falls on people's minds like a stone in a pond. He transcends it but they do not transcend it. But it is part of the very essence of truth that it be transcended. This is why any philosophical system (Descartes, Kant, Hegel) that intends to enclose the world remains at the stage of pure blind pride.* Besides, it must be added that this pride changes into despair

---

*[*Curiosity* (in parallel with ignorance):

1. As *relation to Being*. The curious person: that is *no concern* of his. That is none of his business. Thus the *non-practical* aspect of truth. Or rather: in order to possess being. Reversal.

2. In order to give to others. The *gift* becoming the goal. *In order to communicate.*]

(Hegel). Because if the truth is not supposed to live, then the system is dead truth and the world is *only this*. Riches become poverty. Joy comes from open truth: I have understood the world in its totality and all of it remains to be understood. Because if the truth is stopped, then it is *given* and passivity takes the place of freedom. At the same time, I who deliver myself openly to others with my truth, I, together with my discovery, am transformed by the other's look into an object. What I have seen of Being will be the measure of my subjectivity and, through my very existence, I will be an object for the other.

Therefore we can explain the portion of truth that I have grasped in the world through my *Einstellung*,[49] my complexes and my historical surroundings. Thus revelation itself has an outside, as a free operation of my mind, which escapes me at the very time I freely carry out this revelation. I am paralyzed by an objectivity that I do not know [*ignore*]. This explains the temptation towards pessimism which should be rejected: what I see appears to me as pure, relative *relationship* to my history, my character, my education, etc. In fact, we must hold on firmly to the evidence as absolute evidence that no one can take from us, all the while recognizing that this evidence is paralyzed in its core by the look of others, which defines it but cannot suppress it. Therefore I must accept the fact that anguish as the revealing freedom of an aspect of the world can be *explained* by others in terms of the objective situation of the petty bourgeoisie. But it would be a mistake to believe that it is *relative* to this situation, in other words, that it is a nonrevelatory and purely subjective epiphenomenon. Even though it indeed arises on the basis of the declining petty bourgeoisie and its projects, it is an absolute revelation and absolutely transmits Being.[50]

As far as *universal* truth is concerned, it is a pure abstract statement, that is, the pure index of a permanent possibility, valid for everyone, of freely realizing a certain unveiling. Besides, from this point on, the unveiling is no longer realized and the truth becomes dead-truth or *fact*. Therefore, each living truth that I unveil in itself conceals its own death insofar as it demands to be universalized, that is, insofar as my freedom wants to be freedom in the midst of others' freedom. It *is unto death* (much more so than Heideggerian man). Strictly speaking, it is neither a demand of revealed being as such nor of revelation limited to itself. It is a demand of revealing freedom, which, as freedom, exists only in and through its effort to make the Other be free.

II. We have seen that ignorance is imposed by action.

a) because truth is not *given* but must appear at the end of an operation;

b) because Being is illuminated by the end that-is-not;

c) because the For-itself is not Being and because the independent-Being of the In-itself implies that it is not the consciousness that we acquire of it that makes it be (unlike the For-itself that only exists to the extent that it is conscious of existing). Therefore Being appears always to the revealing For-itself as having already been, and thus first of all and in essence as not having been known [*ignoré*].

But if this applies to the truth presently being verified and which appears on the ground of my not knowing it [*d'ignorance* d'elle] (when I am opening a letter, I *do not know* [ignore] what is in it), it also fits all the truths I will concern myself with, which I know that I will concern myself with, which I know that I cannot stop concerning myself with, because I will live beyond this verification and I will continue to verify *in order to* exist. Therefore *my* truth appears on the ground of ignorance of innumerable other truths, and the interiorization of my finitude, or choice, implies that I *decide* to not know [*ignorer*] in order to know—to not know [*ignorer*] *the rest* in order to know *this*. Consequently, *my* truth has an internal relationship with the ignorance of what is outside of it (even if the outside has only an *external* relationship with it). For example, to resolve this mathematical problem, I decide not to inform myself about the political situation. The relationship between the problem and the situation is external. But the decision to ignore this situation *in order to* verify the problem results in *subjective* ignorance being a freely chosen condition of verification.

In an even more general way, man is not only the being through whom lack of knowledge [*non-savoir*], like knowledge, comes into the world; he is also the being who *must not know* [ignorer] in order to act. Indeed action is the illumination of Being as means in terms of the end, that is, the definition of Being as possible means beginning from a state to-come [*à-venir*] of this same Being. But, precisely because of this structure, Being is first of all unknown and can reveal itself as *in no way* being able to sustain the operational role that we want it to play. Therefore the end is only *possible* and I do not know if I will realize it to the very extent that I ignore Being. This is not only a result of my relationship to Being but a condition of freedom itself. If, indeed, we were to determine the end in terms of the clear knowledge of the means, this would mean that the present produces the future: I choose to eat because I see a knife, fork, and meat on a table. But in this case I am, as a revealing person, a pure intermediary between these objects and their consequences. *Through me* they realize their function and produce their effects with certainty. This is exactly what determinism is. The means encountered would make the end surge up as pure result of its operational function; the end could not be *proposed* but imposed. And, undoubtedly, it happens that the presence of a means suggests the end: I wasn't thirsty, but the sight of this cup of tea suggests drinking. And, in a sense, it is indeed the *ability* to be able to accomplish the action that suggests doing it. But:

1. This means is only suggestive in a world where, even without desire, the possibility of drinking is my own possibility before discovering the means. This is because my organism indeed needs liquids and the kind of thought that can occur to me is, for example: If I drink now, I will not need to drink later when I am busy. Therefore the presence of the means *awakens* a dormant end, within the perspective of other concrete ends. (Economizing time may be the true end and drinking a pure means. I drink now in order to save time

later, to prevent thirst from occurring. The concrete end: a certain operation to be undertaken which determines every perspective in terms of the future.) On the other hand, if we were to suppose that the sight of the means immediately provokes the pursuit of a new end, we would be determined. But even this is absurd. Because the means cannot produce its end if the category of the *end* is not already posited.

A certain conception of aesthetics that presents itself as "tough" and anti-idealist presupposes that the acoustic, verbal, etc., raw material creates the work (the end). The requirements of verse create the thought (Valéry), the needs of the acting company (finding a role for an actress) places Shakespeare in the situation to create Ophelia, the knot in the wood . . . , etc. Undoubtedly, but this is only true from within the perspective of a general thought (*La Jeune Parque*[51] as project, the project of writing about Hamlet's revenge because the previous plays had been successful). And in this case it comes down to this banality: the coefficient of adversity revealed in the *possible* means obliges the artist to seek another means which is farther removed, less easy, and which will make the work more complex and successful. In short, we are dealing with the first stammerings of thinkers who want to be realists and stress the importance of matter, the unexpected, in short, the resistance of the *situation*.

2. If the simple decision to realize *this* end entails the automatic compliance of the *means*, which so many people dream of, the result would be that the means exist only *through* the end and *for* the end. No other relation to the world would be possible except for those prescribed by the end (otherwise the occurrence of a change in the world would risk interrupting the realization in process). In short, the end, instead of illuminating the existent, would in its search for means, produce its own means *ex nihilo*. The end would be creative. Non-being would itself create its own instruments of realization. But, in this case, *either* Mind [*Esprit*] thus reveals itself through the individual person and we no longer have action or freedom, because man himself is a means to realize the end, is impaled on the vector of means-and-ends, is ultimately cre-

ated by the end and suppresses himself in it—*or indeed the individual person, in his gratuitousness, projects an end*. But if it is enough to project an end in order for it to be realized, this means that we find ourselves in the realm of *wish*, or even imagination. But not in that of work. And in this world, no *decision* is possible any more because, since any conception entails its realization, desire can no longer be distinguished from deliberate choice. *Postponement* is impossible, as is the decision to renounce, as is the invention of better means. In short, possibility in general becomes impossible.* I am condemned to see realized [*voir réaliser*] what I think, in short I pass from the free world into the prison world of dreams: it is enough for a possible to be conceived as possible in order for it to become real; there no longer is a distinction between the possible and the real; we find ourselves in a universe where *inevitably* a possible *is* real and, conversely, where reality always remains on the level of the possible.

Therefore action requires the illumination of a reality already being [*déjà étante*] through an end and this reality can reveal itself as obstacle, delay, or obstruction to be overcome. Thus the demand of freedom is that reality *can always be revealed* as contrary to my designs. It goes without saying that if this reality were to reveal itself as absolutely and always contrary, no end would *even* be conceivable *any more:* only a vague dream of the possible ruminated upon beyond Being and bursting like a bubble. Were reality *always* to be propitious or *always* contrary, it would be nothing but a dream. But ignorance is the possibility, not known, that the real is contrary (or, in terms of action: risk). In its being, freedom is the acceptance of *risk;* there is risk only for and through a freedom. And what is being risked, finally, is freedom itself. Because if the *certainty* that reality is always contrary kills freedom, the *possibility* of being killed by an always contrary reality is, on the contrary, posited by freedom. In its surging up freedom posits the possibility that the world renders free-

*Beyond the sensual love of the ways of being, the austere and fundamental love of Being.

dom impossible. And this possibility is not a pure abstract limit because *it is true* that the world can always render certain freedoms impossible (economic crises, slavery) and that it can become such (e.g., destruction of the world) that any freedom becomes henceforth impossible in it. Since freedom cannot impose any claim on being, it is, in principle, a *fact* without basis that my freedom is possible today in the midst of the world.

In this sense, every concrete action that discovers and invents its means with total responsibility is always fully comprehensible *on the ground of chance*, that is, on condition that, all things being equal, the order of the world makes a freedom (or this freedom) possible. But this world order would be the object of a total and detailed knowledge that is denied to me and which, besides, I refuse through the interiorization of my own finitude (the choice of a particular end). Therefore freedom demands basic ignorance of the overall destiny that the world holds for the human enterprise.* This ignorance unveils it as pure freedom in its own eyes, that is, it asserts itself *in any case*, no matter what may be the outcome. On the other hand, this indicates that the means do not dictate the end (realism)—and it is not the attractiveness of the end that exercises its right over the existence of the means (idealism)—but that the end presents and pursues itself outside the *occasion*, whatever may be its outcome and provided that the situation does not appear as *certainly contrary*. Besides, ultimately, freedom can choose to be destroyed by the choice of its own end (desperate resistance) because its failure demonstrates it to be an order that is different from the world order.

Not knowing [*ignorant*] the exact *possibility* of action, human-reality must equally be ignorant of [*ignorer*] not *all* but most of its consequences. The problem presents itself therefore as follows: my choice, as interiorization of my finitude, is the choice of a *completed* end. But, on the other hand, the ob-

---

*[In this case, Mallarmé: a being of chance who denies chance.][52]

ject that is realized in the world has infinite relations with the infinite collection of beings and, besides, since it is realized in the human world, it will be grasped from an infinite series of aspects and will serve as springboard for an infinite series of actions. In reality this is only a possibility: certain acts do not go beyond a certain threshold before they annihilate themselves; others go beyond this threshold, extend themselves in the world and plunge into nothingness; still others are immediately blocked by the interference of other series. But the *possibility* remains that my act will have infinitely infinite consequences. Insofar as it is *my* act, these consequences are mine and I must assume them. But insofar as it is finished, I do not know [*ignore*] them. Therefore a freedom's situation is to assume what it has not done (assumption of the situation) in order to assume what it does not know [*ignore*] (the consequences of its acts). The structure of this assumption (the passage of the act to *the objective*) will not be examined here. It is enough to note this ignorance or claim of the infinite by finitude itself. Choice is interiorization of finitude; the assumption of the consequences of choice (assumption made in ignorance and in the future) is interiorization of the infinite.

This does not at all mean that action must not be a decision of finitude: I can be interested only in a finite number of consequences (I act from the perspective of this generation and the next one) but this very decision implies a ground of infinitude: through it I decide in total freedom what my relationships will be with the infinite consequences, I take full responsibility for shouldering in indifference the responsibilities of these consequences, beyond a certain limit. In short, I accept answering for this indifference before a tribunal to come. (This means that I establish a *relationship* with these consequences: I consider them, in any case, as being of lesser interest. Thus I assume them, in any case, as having to be accepted as they are. And if later on I have to be confronted with one of them, I must be able to say: "At least this is my project, even if it often fails. I regret nothing or I would do it again if it had to be done again.") But there again there is a risk because, whatever may be my decision to ignore certain consequences or to assume them *all*, there is a possibility that the unforeseen consequences will destroy the foreseen consequences: by wanting to ensure the happiness of this social group, of this person, I have posited an end that I have attained, but the ultimate consequences of that end destroy this very happiness. In short, the risk affects not just the realization of this end (adversity of means) and not just the distant consequences of this end, but also its immediate consequences.

Freedom must assume a heritage; whatever it does it leaves behind a heritage. It neither knows precisely what this heritage will be, nor what the heirs will do with it, nor what these heirs will be like. It knows neither if it will attain its end, nor if the attained end will destroy itself. But it is from the perspective of this risk and of this ignorance that it historializes itself and unveils being in *Truth*.[53] And the situation of freedom is such that, in any case, it takes the risk, even if it wants to avoid the risk (*Appointment in Samarra*).[54] If it struggles to avoid risk, it cuts its relationships with it and can no longer claim responsibility for an accident that happens, which consequently comes to it in the form of *fate*. If, in order to protect my life, I avoid taking the plane or train, quitting or joining a party, then death caused by typhoid or cholera, as totally external to my project, is fate. If, on the other hand, by means of the above commitments, I accept the risk of death as permanent (in ignorance), death through sickness is the contingent form that a risk takes that is foreseen and assumed: it is human. Ignorance as the underside of Truth is necessity for the freedom of risking our very existence, in a world that can contradict it radically. Therefore Truth appears on the ground of a world that can render truth impossible. Through its very existence it struggles and affirms itself against this possibility of its impossibility. By seeing what I see I make the possibility surge up that no vision will ever again be possible any place in the world, but at the same time I create the impossibility that this temporal moment (with its three ek-static dimensions), in which the Truth illuminated the world, did not take place.

Thus *an absolute* appears. Truth is an absolute on the ground of a supreme risk.

III. But all these kinds of ignorances that we have just examined, although essentially determining Truth in its nature, are ignorances that temporalize themselves and will pass from ignorance to knowledge. I will know certain consequences of my acts, which I momentarily do not know [*ignore*]; other persons will know others; they will only be important in *being revealed,* thus in becoming truths. It is only my finitude and the necessity for truth to temporalize itself, because nothing is given to human freedom, that constitutes this horizon of ignorance around me. But there are, besides this, structural ignorances, that is, ignorances that will never temporalize themselves into truth. They result from the fact that man, carrying truth everywhere, creates zones of *possible truth* in regions where verifiability is forbidden to him. This means that he anticipates, through his very existence, through questions without possible answers. This does not mean that these questions are fantasies or illusions, nor that they are purely subjective questions that result from an a priori structure of knowledge. Not at all: these questions are relationships to Being and constitute Being as susceptible of being verified. There *is* a truth to these questions. But at the same time this truth will remain truth *for no one.* I will give only one example, which will plunge us into the very heart of this necessary ignorance.

Man grasps the Other as signifying object, and through the very death of the Other the truth of the Other's life surges up as destiny. The For-itself knows, on account of the evidence of the Other, that his own life will one day have its truth as a Destiny. And this is not yet a radical ignorance, in the sense that even though the objective meaning of my life escapes me, it can exist for others, and I can prefigure in my behavior and in risk the meaning that I would like it to have. We are already grasping a truth that has meaning only in the exteriority of *Mitsein.* The *age* in which I live has itself an objective meaning which it creates by being alive and which escapes it because it creates it *for others*. Yet the question of its meaning [*signification*] is *alive* for it because it knows that it will have this meaning and it seeks to grasp it in advance. But the very manner in which it seeks to grasp it will contribute to giving it its meaning in the eyes of future generations. For example, the attempt to interpret social phenomena in economic terms will perhaps appear to our descendants as the dominant *intellectual* characteristic of our age: in short, the material truth unveiled by an age which is in the process of finding itself will become intellectual truth for the next generation.

Thus the age is truth for itself but it is a truth that is not known [*ignorée*]. Yet there will be a revealed truth of this age. Therefore, because the spirit of the age is a *detotalized* totality, the truth of a group exists always for another group of *one* individual. Consequently, as a detotalized *totality*, the spirit of the age poses the question of its *whole* meaning. Insofar as there will be totalization of man (for example as catastrophic end of History), insofar as this death of the human is immediately and always *possible* as possibility of the impossibility of freedom, the human totality is perpetually present to any person. If it were *totalizable totality*, that is, a human consciousness that is one and universal, it would be totality as consciousness of itself. Thus it would attain the region where Being and Truth are one. But as *detotalized* totality the destiny of mankind always appears to an *other*. Totalization is always made by *one man*, and he totalizes the past up to this day with *all present human beings*. But this totalization remains subjective and must in turn rejoin History in the form of *one* historical totalization through an arbitrary stopping of the clock. Yet the death of mankind would be a *real* totalization through the absolute stopping of the clock. And the perpetual awareness, even though not thematic, of this stopping thus causes the anticipation of a truth of humankind to surge up in everyone. Insofar as a totalization of humankind is always possible, *there is a truth of humankind*. Humankind has a destiny, History has a meaning (even if it is only a series of catastrophic absurdities, because then, since man is the being through whom meaning comes into the world, the meaning of History would be the impossibility of a meaning for the being who confers meaning on Being).

But this meaning of History could only appear to a being situated *outside* of History, since all understanding of History is itself historical and temporalizes itself from within the perspective of a future, and, thus, of new ends. After all, we are not necessarily dealing with a God or a demiurge—it could be a man who has remained outside of the human realm. In any case it is necessary to have *someone close the eyes of humanity.* And that someone being impossible in principle, man is the worker of a truth that no one will ever know. That is, the finished For-itself *passes into Being* and because of this collapses into the night. But the For-itself, because its existence is enlightenment of Being, has as project its own illumination beyond death and becomes thereby *illuminable.* Indeed, it should be remarked that the totalization of the human would undoubtedly not require in principle a different intelligence and means of information than ours: were we to furnish a contemporary group of scientists with totalizing information about the life of an isolated human species that has disappeared, then it would undoubtedly be able to gradually discover its meaning. What renders Truth impossible is that man makes History and that he is still making it while knowing it. Thus man, by the very fact that he is free, is haunted by an absolute truth of man that exists as a virtuality that is perfectly accessible, which is like the Platonic ideal serving as motor to the discipline of history and which, however, escapes it in principle. Man is *ignorance of self.* He is ignorance of self because he makes what he is and he needs *someone else* to illuminate what he has been. He is ignorance of self because he is not nature but destiny, because man's adventure is not finished as long as one man remains alive to confer his meaning on it, and afterward it collapses into nothingness, lacking witnesses. Therefore the being through whom the light comes to illuminate Being is both pure lucidity (beyond truth) as subjective consciousness and pure darkness (on this side of it) as Destiny.[55]

77

For example, let us consider this classic question: Why does man live? This very question arises because man is the being through whom the *For* [Pour] comes into the world. But this does not mean that he carries a *category* in his mind, the category of finality that would have no a priori right on the world. The *Why* comes into the world through action and freedom. Therefore the being through whom the *Why* surges up in the world turns back on it in order to raise the *Why*. But the subjective answer of the isolated man is clear: indeed there is a *Why* of his being, but this *Why* cannot have been given to him because his own freedom is the foundation of every *Why*. The *Why* of my existence is the ultimate project and the essential possibility towards which I project myself. The *Why* of my existence surges up in my very existence. But because of the existence of the Others, and particularly of future generations, the *Why* of my existence is given as *the objective reason* for my being-in-itself. I surge up *at the right moment in order to*, and the meaning [*signification*] of my being is grasped in its end-oriented [*finaliste*] aspect in terms of the entire age. The *Why* that my existence projects ahead [*jette en avant*] is replaced by my function in the age, and it is not necessarily the same (quite the contrary). I now become *objective*. I receive my *Why* from the age that I express. At that moment, I receive my *Why* as a destiny. ("Mr. X's work, which by the way, is execrable, is precious because it demonstrates . . . , etc.") Ultimately we come back to the raison d'être of the man who would be the *Why* grasped, as destiny of man, by a transcendent who is present at the end of History. Thus am I inhabited by a *Why* of which I am ignorant [*ignore*] (this is the meaning both of Kafka's anxieties and Hegel's "cunning of reason"). The cunning of reason has no place in subjectivity as free choice: it is quite simply the passage to the objective. Thus, in choosing my destiny, I will act *as* a Frenchman, as a bourgeois, as a man of the twentieth century, etc. My objectivity haunts my subjectivity as a reality that is not known [*ignorée*].

The identification with the body's impulses that characterizes the rural population of the nineteenth century is for them an absolute way of life. For us it becomes an *object*. A reversal of positions has happened: the *Why* that was *to come* is now the transcendent meaning of the series of my objective manifestations. Therefore there is a *Why* of man *made by man* through a subjective choice of his fundamental *Why*, not known [*ignoré*] precisely by the one who chooses because it is nothing but the passage to the objective of the choice that existed subjectively. My free choice to exile myself, objectified in the emigration statistics, reverses itself and I become the victim of a great migratory force that pushes me along. "In the eighteenth century the movement of emigration becomes stronger in relationship to . . . , etc." Or a particular action that I undertake, which is objectified and linked to others, becomes "a sign of the bourgeoisie's decline." Thus everything happens as if consciousness were mystifying and as if the social and economic dimensions were the unconsciousness of the historical agent.

I distinguish historiality from historization. To me historiality is the project that the For-itself makes of itself in History: by deciding to undertake the coup d'état of the 18th Brumaire, Bonaparte historializes himself. And I call historization the passing of historialization to the objective. It results in historicity, or belonging objectively to an age. It is evident that historialization is the objective transcendence of the age and that, on the other hand, historicity is pure expression of the age. Historization is the outcome of transcendence from the point of view of a subsequent age, or the passage from historialization to historicity. Thus there is perpetual mystification. And for a transcendent and noncommitted consciousness, completed history would be the historicity of all of mankind, that is, the free historialization of men turned into congealed Destiny. We make one kind of history and *another one is written*. Kaiser Wilhelm II decides to struggle against British imperialism and this historialization falls back into historicity: through Wilhelm II a civil war began on a world scale, opposing the proletariat to the propertied classes. But what must be understood is that it is in historialization that the concrete absolute, and the unveiling of truth to the absolute-subject, reside. The mistake is in seeing an epi-phenomenon of historicity there, instead of seeing historicity as the meaning conferred on my project insofar as it is no longer lived or concrete, but pure abstract in-itself.

Therefore we must make ourselves historical against a mystifying history, that is, historialize ourselves against historicity. This can be done only by clinging to the finitude of the lived experience as interiorization. It is not by attempting to transcend our age towards the eternal or towards a future of which we have no grasp that we will escape from historicity; on the contrary, it is by accepting to transcend ourselves only in and through this age, and by seeking in the age itself the concrete ends that we intend to propose to ourselves. If I know myself as, and want to be, part of my age, I transcend it towards itself and not towards an age that has not yet arrived. I most certainly do not escape from historization, but it is a *minimal* historization: only of my age. By not pretending to be living with my grandchildren, I keep them from judging me by their standards. By giving them my act as a *proposition*, in order that they may do with it what they want, I escape the risk that they do with it something other than I wanted.

APPENDIX
NEW OUTLINE

Introduction: Ethics and History
1. What is Ethics?
2. Necessity of morality

3. Morality and historicity $\begin{cases} \text{Kant} \\ \text{Hegel} \\ \text{Marx} \\ \text{Trotsky} \end{cases}$

—The Antinomy $\begin{cases} \text{technique and political necessity} \\ \text{ethical necessities} \end{cases}$

4. What is historicity: subjective-objective;
5. Morality (historialization) and historization.
   Historialization = concrete morality.
   Concrete Future/Abstract Future.

Therefore I am searching for an ethics *for the present*, that is, the fact of total historialization. I am trying to elucidate the choice that a man can make of himself and of the world in 1948.

This choice presupposes $\begin{cases} \text{1. an ontological horizon} \\ \text{2. a historical context} \\ \text{3. a concrete future} \end{cases}$

Part One: The ontological horizon: *pure* reflection.[56]
Part Two: The historical fact of *alienation.*
Part Three: The choice of a concrete future.

The discovery of the 3 temporal ek-stases occurs in the movement of the passage from the abstract to the concrete.

81

1. *Eternity* as abstract reality of the essences and of nature, as substance. Temporality = appearance (the feudal conception of time).

2. *The abstract past:*

—The lived past of the eighteenth century (feudalism, absolute monarchy, etc.).

—The projected past: the past of the *Greeks and Romans.* ABSTRACT.

3. *The abstract present* (18th century): *The concrete past has been achieved.*

—The present and *analysis:* the synthesis temporalizes itself. In itself the analysis is affirmation of the present.

—The present and eternity (the noble savage).

—Ethics for *the moment.*

—*Concrete present:* the *Untergang*[57] of the "Ancien Régime" with the Revolution that is on the horizon.

4. 19th century: the concrete achieved; we live the present from within the perspective of a *true* past: the Revolution becomes *concrete* past for the people of the 19th century. The meaning of the Revolution is that it confers a concrete past: coincidence of the lived past and of the represented past.

—The *abstract future:* indefinite progress, end of History, Comte's conception of society, or, in the case of Kant, endless progress beyond the phenomenal world.

20th century: the discovery of the concrete future, due to despair with an abstract future (failures *discover* the concrete future as a potential for barbarism—Marx—etc.).

The concrete future or the future of the age: defined by the most remote future mapped out by a concrete project (atomic energy, etc.).

The middle classes' mediocrity as a phenomenon of *resentment.*

NOTES

1. Sartre's thesis of conversion is developed in *Cahiers pour une morale* (Paris, 1983); see pp. 448–531; *Notebooks for an Ethics* (Chicago, 1992), pp. 471–554. For Sartre, to state that inauthenticity is a mode of common being is to state that, in order to escape from contingency, the primordial human project seeks perpetually to become one with one's "character," one's social situation, one's possessions, etc. . . . *Accomplice reflection* is the means by which the for-itself tries to make itself in-itself-for-itself. These attempts remain futile: I cannot convince myself in a lasting manner that I *am* such and such. On the other hand, the look of the other unifies, whether I wish it or not, the totality of my behaviors and tends to consider me as a *being*. This is the origin of alienation, either because I do everything to identify myself with that being that the look of the other returns to me, or because I seek to escape from it. *Pure reflection* is the conscious grasping of that fundamental failure of accomplice reflection; it is the first step towards what Sartre calls *conversion*, or the project of calling oneself into question as *existent*, instead of seeking to congeal oneself in *being* [être]. It is the acceptance of the fact that the mode of being of the existent is "diasporatic."

It may be worthwhile to establish a parallel in tone between the idea of authenticity as expressed on the one hand in *Being and Nothingness* and in the pages, cited above, of the *Notebooks* and, on the other hand, in Heidegger's conception. As far as original inauthenticity is concerned, Sartre stresses the desire of the for-itself to *congeal* itself in the in-itself; Heidegger stresses the *agitation* of human reality as a *They* ["on," "das Man"], his wandering from entity [*étant*] to entity [*étant*]. As far as the authenticity of action in history is concerned, Sartre stresses "the transformation of gratuitousness into absolute freedom," finitude as the necessity for this freedom and creation; Heidegger stresses the inheritance of past possibilities (repetition, choice of heroes) and their re-absorption into future possibility with death as the appropriate possibility at the horizon of all action. See Martin Heidegger, "On the Essence of Truth," *Basic Writings* (New York, 1976), p. 118. (A. E.-S.)

2. By "doctrine of historicity" Sartre has in mind an ethics which would be based on an anchoring of human-reality in an age, a place, a community. The moral options would have to be constituted in the meaning of this anchorage, leaving undetermined, from an ethical point of view, relations with the rest of the world. (A. E.-S.) But see Sartre, pp. 79–80 above and note 53 below. (A. van den H., R. A.)

3. In his preface to Roger Stéphane's *Portrait de l'aventurier* included in *Situations*, VI (Paris, 1964), Sartre analyzes the ontological horizon of the adventurer and stresses the latter's attraction to Nothingness. (A. E.-S.)

4. In the last pages of this text a distinction will be made between historization and historialization. (A. E.-S.)

5. Moral conversion, as the passage from accomplice reflection to pure reflection, is by definition individual, even though it modifies the relationship to the other. But for an ethics to exist, the human community must recognize it as its own. Here, therefore, the author seems to distance himself from the idea that an ethics can be founded solely on conversion: since the original project is fascination with Being (Being-in-itself-for-itself of inauthenticity), we must take this love of Being into account. One possibility comes to mind: not convincing men to renounce *being*, but to posit Being as a desirable and always receding end of History, for itself and for all men. (A. E.-S.)

6. This allusion to *mystery* confirms that Sartre had clearly begun to read "On the Essence of Truth" (*De l'Essence de la vérité*, [Paris, 1948], Alphonse De Waehlens' translation of Heidegger's *Von Wesen der Wahrheit* [Frankfurt, 1954]) at the time he was writing these pages. (It is difficult to say whether he was aware of this lecture earlier. Although published in French in 1948, it had been presented in 1930.) In it Heidegger argues that *Dasein* (or human-reality), formal source of the disclosure of being [*être*], discloses entities [*les étants*] as such and, in the same movement, conceals the fact that entity [*étant*] in totality raises questions and it forgets this dissimulation. This forgetting does not prevent a certain presence of what the author calls *mystery*. For Heidegger, *Dasein* is defined as being divided between error (forgetting of self and of Being [*être*] in the discovery and the manipulation of specific entities [*étants*]) and the forgotten mystery. (A. E.-S.)

7. See *Being and Nothingness*, pp. l–lvi (Introduction, III: "The Prereflective Cogito and the Being of the *Percipere*"). (A. E.-S., R. A.)

8. See Paul Ricoeur's distinction between *présenter* and *présentifier* in his translation of Husserl, *Idées* (Paris, 1989), p. 22, n. 11. See also *L'Etre et le Néant*, pp. 168, 211. (A. van den H.)

9. See "The Essence of Truth," pp. 130–32. (A. van den H.)

10. See *De l'Essence de la vérité*, p. 75. (A. van den H.)

11. This remark is related to pp. 9–10: the unveiling mission of the For-itself is paralyzed if it becomes fascinated by what the generation after the next one will make of what it unveils, or if it pretends to unveil only truths that are valid for centuries that are yet to come. (A. E.-S.)

12. Sartre has inadvertently moved from one hypothesis (a final *sub-*

jectivity) to another (a final *generation*) but this does not change the argument. We must not forget that he was reflecting upon these concepts at the same time as he was writing this first draft, without crossing anything out. (A. E.-S.)

13. The writing on this page is a little vague. The search for truth is intended to be totalizing, but of course the totality will not be attained and this is not even desirable. Because if a "melodic" end awaits us at the end of History, the meaning of which would be outside of us, whether it be a God who is its master or whether one supposes the existence of a last generation who knows, so to speak, History's last word, then we are only the blind means by which this meaning comes about, and all search for truth is futile. But if, while accepting our finitude, we delimit for ourselves an end of History, without theological or scientific extrapolation, truth and historical action become possible. This question is taken up again in the last pages: in fact it is the conclusion of the present work. (A. E.-S.)

14. *Les Temps Modernes*, June 1948. This text, written in 1946, had a great impact in France and abroad. The English version appears in *The Selected Prose Writings of Jean-Paul Sartre*, ed. Michel Contat and Michel Rybalka, trans. Richard McCleary (Evanston, 1974). (A. E.-S., R. A.)

15. *Being and Nothingness*, pp. lx–lxii. (R. A.)

16. The for-itself constitutes itself *as not being* the in-itself. See ibid., pp. 21–45. (A. E.-S., R. A.)

17. Pure being-near. (A. E.-S.)

18. See *Cahiers pour une morale*, pp. 250–56; *Notebooks for an Ethics*, pp. 240–45. (A. E.-S., R. A.)

19. The author is in fact William James: *Pragmatism* (Cambridge, Mass., 1975).

20. For what follows, see *Being and Nothingness*, pp. 577–80, *Qu'est-ce que la littérature?*, *Situations, II* (Paris, 1948); trans. Bernard Frechtman, *What Is Literature?* (New York, 1949), pp. 51–53. (R. A.)

21. Heidegger, "On the Essence of Truth," p. 130. (R. A., A. van den H.)

22. See Jean de La Fontaine, *Complete Fables* (Evanston, 1988). (R. A.)

23. Henri Bergson, *Matter and Memory* (New York, 1988). (R. A.)

24. Sartre raised this question in his *War Diaries* (pp. 199, 293), about an article by Roger Caillois on "the myth of the big city" ("Paris, mythe moderne," *La Nouvelle revue française*, May 1937). Can we realize our *being-in* Paris, for example, or isn't it pure representation? Also, isn't adventure *unrealizable?* (A. E.-S.)

25. Sartre adopts the term from Heidegger; it appears in "On the Essence of Truth," p. 128, with the following translator's note: "This variant of the word Existenz indicates the ecstatic character of freedom, its standing outside itself." (R. A.)

26. *Cahiers pour une morale*, pp. 347–50. In these pages Sartre elaborates in detail on ignorance (see the thematic index); *Notebooks for an Ethics*, pp. 334–37. (A. E.-S, A. van den H., R. A.)

27. Without any warning, Sartre is apparently resuming a discussion from the *Notebooks for an Ethics*. Note that in doing so, he has changed the situation being described from two others in that text, one in which he is running alone (pp. 334–35) and one in which he is observing someone running (pp. 336–38), into one in which he is being chased. (A. van den H., R. A.)

28. See Edmund Husserl, *Ideas* (New York, 1931), analytic index, p. 443. (A. van den H.)

29. *Epoché*, a phenomenological term first used by Edmund Husserl, refers to the suspension of belief in the existence of the world. Putting the world "into parentheses" allows consciousness to focus on the phenomena it contains and, later, on its own acts of bestowing meaning on the world. See Husserl, *Ideas*, p. 436. As Hazel Barnes says, "Sartre, of course, does not follow this procedure since his task is to examine consciousness in-the-world" (*Being and Nothingness*, p. 630). It is worth noting that Sartre uses the term during his first encounters with Husserl, for example, in *La Transcendance de l'ego: Esquisse d'une description phénoménologique* (Paris, 1965); *The Transcendence of the Ego: An Existentialist Theory of Consciousness*, trans. Forrest Williams and Robert Kirkpatrick (New York, 1957), pp. 35, 113–14. (R. A.)

30. Lived experience [*le vécu*]. See Ricoeur's glossary in Husserl, *Idées*, p. 522. (A. van den H., R. A.)

31. See Plato, *Republic*, trans. Francis MacDonald Cornford (New York, 1945), Book V, 474–80; pp. 179–89. (R. A.)

32. This passage can be compared with Heidegger's position in "On the Essence of Truth." Let us go back to the notion that Sartre just rejected insofar as it supposedly defined *Dasein* (or human-reality) in its initial relationship to truth, the notion of *mystery*, i.e., *Dasein*'s "concealment" of Being [*étant*] in totality, thus the question of Being, and the dissimulation of that concealment. For Sartre, whose perspective here is the search for a moral prescription for our acts, recognizing mystery resolves nothing: man runs the risk of passing from the futile agitation described by Heidegger to empty contemplation, to a paralysis of action. Thus his question: *why* this dissimulation? Notice that for Heidegger *Dasein*, in order to arrive at the truth of Being, will have to renounce limiting itself to "current reality which is capable of being dominated," while, for Sartre, the existent is the living and practical organism, "the man of need," and as such he comes to veil or to ignore Being [*Etre*]. But since Being [*Etre*] is not adapted to man, the progressive and uninterrupted verification of particular beings [*étants*] is necessary in order for human-reality to continue to exist. (A. E.-S.)

33. Undoubtedly Sartre's first formulation of a theme that will play an important role in the *Critique of Dialectical Reason*: the antagonism of praxes against a background of scarcity. Note that here an equal emphasis is placed on *sharing*. (A. E.-S., R. A.)

34. See *L'Etre et le Néant*, p. 190. (A. van den H.)

35. Sartre had already elaborated on this theme in his discussion of Kaiser

Wilhelm II's disability as presented in Emil Ludwig's biography of the Kaiser. He stressed the significance of Wilhelm's atrophied left arm for the development of his psyche, his militarism, and his ambivalent attitude towards Great Britain (see Sartre, *Les Carnets de la drôle de guerre* [Paris, 1983]; trans. Quintin Hoare, *War Diaries*, pp. 301–19). Sartre also establishes a link with his own disability, his being walleyed. It prevents him from being a scientist but it also makes him want to seduce others intellectually. Sartre develops the same theme but in a "Third-World" political and economic context in *L'Engrenage* (Paris, 1948); trans. Mervyn Saville, *In the Mesh* (London, 1954). (A. van den H.)

36. This and the following is an early formulation of the theme of counterfinality, which will be central in *Critique of Dialectical Reason*. See Introduction, above, p. xxxiii. (R. A.)

37. This is discussed in *Being and Nothingness*, pp. 194–204. (R. A.)

38. In medicine, invagination refers to the telescoping of an organ in the manner of a pouch. See Benjamin F. Miller and Claire Brackman Keane, *Encyclopedia and Dictionary of Medicine and Nursing* (Philadelphia, 1972), p. 495. (A. van den H.)

39. See *Psychology of Imagination*, pp. 210–11, and Introduction above, n. 8, p. xxxvi. (R. A.)

40. See Sartre's striking discussion of the angel as an abstract ideal person in his discussion of alternatives to Stalin in *Critique de la raison dialectique*, II (Paris, 1985), p. 220; trans. Quintin Hoare, *Critique of Dialectical Reason* (London, 1991), II, p. 209. See Ronald Aronson, *Sartre's Second Critique* (Chicago, 1987), p. 159. (R. A.)

41. Marcel Proust, *Remembrance of Things Past*, vol. 2: *The Guermantes Way. Cities of the Plain* (New York, 1981), pp. 778–809. See also *Being and Nothingness*, p. 164. (A. van den H.)

42. See Heidegger, "On The Essence of Truth," p. 125. (R. A.)

43. In evolution: transformation in the same, constant direction. See André Lalonde, *Vocabulaire technique et critique de la Philosophie* (Paris, 1947), pp. 300, 1167. In medicine: the mechanical transmission of disease germs from an infected person to a well person. See Miller and Keane, p. 1018. (A. van den H., R. A.)

44. Truth indicating itself. (A. van den H.)

45. It may be worthwhile to again compare Sartre's point of view on authenticity with that of Heidegger's, because after all, this authenticity (of the being-there or human-reality) has to have a relationship with truth. The notion of *alter ego* seems to correspond to that of *repetition* and *fidelity* in *Being and Time* in making things more complex and less fatalistic (we are using Henri Corbin's terminology from *Qu'est-ce que la métaphysique?* [*What Is Metaphysics?*] (Paris, 1937) because Sartre usually uses the terminology of this translation). Sartre is not happy with the notion of *repetition* as the "possibility of existence having-been-a-presence," as a guarantee of a project's authenticity—whether that existence has been mine or, more cor-

rectly, inherited from ancestors, even if Heidegger is careful to point out that we are dealing with a reaction to this possibility and not with a simple repetition of the past. His conception preserves, through an apprehension in movement (tearing away—continuity), the unique character of each act and therefore a certain relationship of human-reality with the absolute and, as he says here, "an outline of the infinite" within an ethics of finitude. Obviously this also pertains to the unveiling act, and this vocation of truth to infinity will be confirmed later on.

Let us recall here, because it is related to their different conceptions of authenticity, Sartre's rejection of Heidegger's *being-for-death* as structure of human-reality and, insofar as any authentic act would occur under the sign of death, human-reality being caught or indeed smothered between past possibilities to be reactivated and anticipating death as its *own* unique possibility. Sartre criticizes this concept in *Being and Nothingness* (part 4, chap. 1, esp. pp. 531–53). For Sartre, on the other hand, death "is the always possible nihilation of my possibles, it is outside of my possibilities and therefore I can not wait for it; that is, I can not thrust myself towards it as towards one of my possibilities. Death can not therefore belong to the ontological structure of the for-itself" (p. 545). (A. E.-S.)

46. See *Being and Nothingness*, pp. 579–80. (A. E.-S., A. van den H.)

47. A central term of Hegelian thought, *aufgehoben* has three simultaneous layers of meaning: annulled or cancelled, transcended [*dépassé*] or gone beyond, and preserved. See R. D. Laing and D. G. Cooper, *Reason and Violence* (London, 1964), pp. 13–14. (R. A.)

48. Here also, "the other that I will be." (A. E.-S.)

49. My position. (A. E.-S.)

50. We must not forget that when Sartre was writing these lines, he was being ferociously attacked by Communist ideologists. They rejected his entire philosophy as the demoralizing product of moribund petty-bourgeois thought that opposed itself to the "historical process." Today the dominant tendency is towards a psychoanalytic, or even psychopathological, approach to his works. In any case, whatever our point of view, a scientific approach towards the text is required. It has to be treated as raw material that is revealing in spite of itself and at the expense of its explicit meaning, which would then become obsolete. Obviously, Sartre is referring to his own case here, and it is through his philosophy itself that he is reacting to efforts at its potential reification. (A. E.-S.)

51. A poem by Paul Valéry (Paris, 1974); see *The Collected Works of Paul Valéry* (New York, 1958). (A. van den H., R. A.)

52. Stéphane Mallarmé, "Igitur," *Oeuvres complètes* (Paris, 1945), pp. 433–56. (A. van den H.)

53. *Historial* and *s'historialiser* are used by Henri Corbin in his translation of Heidegger's *Qu'est-ce que la métaphysique?* See his foreword, pp. 17–18; see also pp. 50, 57, 59, 60. (A. van den H., R. A.)

54. This novel by John O'Hara appeared in the United States in 1934 and in France in 1948. (A. E.-S., R. A.)

55. Sartre will again deal with the question of the meaning of History in the light of dialectical reason. See *Critique of Dialectical Reason*, I, p. 805–18 (on the possibility of a totalization without a totalizer), and especially volume II. (A. E.-S.)

56. See note 1 above. (A. E.-S.)

57. The decline. (A. E.-S.)

INDEX

A

Absolute subject, 4–8, 26, 53, 54, 80
Abstract man, 58
Aesthetics, "tough" and anti-idealist, 70
Archimedes, 10, 13, 14–15, 26, 64
Atomic theory, 24
Aufgehoben, 63, 88 n. 47
Authenticity and inauthenticity, 1, 2, 30, 46, 83 n. 1, 84 n. 5, 87 n. 45

B

Being and Nothingness, viii, ix, xi, xii, xiv, xv, xvi, xvii, xxviii, xxix, xxxi, xxxiv, xxxvi n. 6, xxxvii n. 11, n. 12, n. 16, xxxix n. 26, xliii, xliv, 3, 13, 83 n. 1, 84 n. 7, 85 n. 15, 85 n. 20, 86 n. 29, 86 n. 34, 88 n. 45, 88 n. 46
Bergson, Henri, 23, 34, 85 n. 23
Blanchot, Maurice, 31
Bonaparte, Napoleon, 79
Broglie, Louis de, 10
Brunschvicg, Léon, xxv

C

Caillois, Roger, 85 n. 24
Christians and Christian ideology, 27

Cogen-Solal, Annie, x
Cogito, 4
Comte, Auguste, 82
Condemned of Altona, The, xi
Consciousness, 3, 6, 9–11, 13–14, 17, 21–22, 29, 38, 44–48, 55, 56; nonthetic, 11, 14
Corbin, Henri, 87 n. 45, 88 n. 53
Counterfinality, of matter, xxxiii, xxxiv
Critique of Dialectical Reason; xi, xv, xxxi, xxxii, xxxiii, xxxvii n. 13, xl nn. 42, 44, xliii, xlv, xlviii: 86 n. 33, 87 n. 40, 88 n. 55

D

Dasein, xxix, 84 n. 6, 86 n. 32
Death, xix, 10, 11–12, 26, 34, 35, 37–38, 74; theory of 13, 88 n. 45
Descartes, René, xxiii, 64, 66; Cartesian analytic geometry, 63; mechanics, 64
Detotalized totality, 7, 26, 64. *See also* Totality
Deviation, xxxiii
Dirty Hands, xii
Disclosing, xxix. *See also* Revealing; Unveiling

91